Dear
Ben,

Happy Cooking,
EATING
AND
DRINKING

Regards
Mark Chan
TAH

FLAVORS OF MY WORLD

A CULINARY TOUR THROUGH 25 COUNTRIES

MANEET CHAUHAN

WITH DOUG SINGER

PHOTOGRAPHS BY QUENTIN BACON

Favorite Recipes® Press

SOUTHWESTERN PUBLISHING GROUP

NASHVILLE, TENNESSEE

Flavors of My World
A Culinary Tour Through 25 Countries
Maneet Chauhan with Doug Singer

SW® SOUTHWESTERN Publishing Group

P. O. Box 305142
Nashville, Tennessee 37230
1-800-358-0560

Photography © by Quentin Bacon

Krista Ruane—Food Stylist
Maryann Pomeranz—Assistant Food Stylist
Jennifer Daoust—Kitchen Assistant

Library of Congress Control Number:
2013933286
ISBN: 978-0-87197-579-9

Editorial Director: Mary Cummings
Project Editor: Tanis Westbrook
Recipe Editor: Nicki Pendleton Wood, CCP
Book Design: Sheri Ferguson

Manufactured in the United States of America
First Printing: 2013

BLACK ROCK SALT

RED CHILE POWDER

SAFFRON

INDIAN CINNAMON

CINNAMON

STAR ANISE

BLACK MUSTARD SEED

WHOLE RED CHILES

CORIANDER SEEDS

AJWAIN

TANDOORI MASALA

CHANNA MASALA

GARAM MASALA

KOKUM

CHAAT MASALA

MARIGOLD FLOWER

AMCHOOR

CANDIED AMLA

HING

DRIED ROSEBUDS

JAGGERY

preface

When you have no personal experience with something, you commonly perceive it as either really easy, or really difficult. I thought that writing a cookbook would be the former. Dream up delicious combinations, develop recipes, test those recipes, regale with stories about my life and culinary journey, have pictures taken, talk to a publisher, get the book printed, and "Voila!" I have a book. If it were only that simple! My first book has been a labor of love: a symphony of moving parts with so many people coming together in perfect harmony.

They say that for something to happen, everything in the universe must come together to make it possible. That's exactly what transpired with this book. Working with Doug as a co-author has been an amazing ride. His input, honest feedback, and the zeal to see this book in our hands as soon as possible made him the perfect person with whom to work—I could not have asked for a better partner! Thank you, Doug, for assisting me in transforming a figment of my imagination into a real, tangible, and beautiful book. I am very proud of us.

Our experience was rife with discovery, serendipity, and education. In Nashville to scout locations for a new restaurant, we took advantage of being in the Music City to meet with the team at the Southwestern Publishing Group. I was completely charmed by their southern hospitality and professionalism, and they have made each and every step simple and extremely pleasant.

Working through them with world-class photographer extraordinaire Quentin Bacon, whose resume includes Michelle Obama, Ina Garten, Mario Batali, Laurent Torendale, Masaharu Morimoto, Gordon Ramsay, and many more, and his team was incredible. His assistant and Graphic Designer Kristen Walther was instrumental, as were veteran food stylist Krista Ruane and her team, assistant food stylist Maryann Pomeranz, and kitchen assistant Jennifer Daoust. Their artistic style truly captured the beauty of these dishes and drinks. Prop stylist Bette Blau over and over magically produced just the right plate, glass, spoon, and surface for each and every shot, including conjuring a molinillo (a somewhat obscure tool used to hand-froth liquids) for the atole shot just like magic out of thin air.

I would like to extend a heartfelt thanks to Ted Allen for the wonderful Foreword. His words mean the world to me, and each and every episode of *Chopped* that I shoot is a memorable day for me. His insight into food is amazing, and I am honored to have him be a part of this project.

This project certainly would not have been possible without the people around me who have been there for me and waited patiently for this book. The blessings of G.M., Shreeji, and Babaji made this a reality, yet there are so many people who are directly responsible for my success. Starting with my parents, Gur Iqbal and Hardeep Chauhan, who have always supported me in my dreams and goals, despite the fact that I kept them (and they claim I still do) on their toes; my sister Reeti Chauhan, who has had more faith in my success than I have at times; my husband, Vivek Deora, who lovingly supports me and constantly challenges me to be better and push myself; Vivek's mom (and luckily now mine) Shashi Deora, whose strength is an inspiration. Our entire families, whose constant efforts, support, and belief in me has kept me going and finishing with friends, colleagues, and each and every person who has touched my life—each encounter has been an experience that has made me stronger and richer.

To my niece Inika and my nephews Vansh, Aarav, and Jai, please know that whatever you set your heart and mind to, you can achieve it.

Last but not least I have to thank my precious daughter, Shagun, for enriching my life. With her little head full of curls, her constant curiosity about this new world unfolding around her, her perpetual discovery mode, her unguarded open-hearted laugh, her trusting eyes, her "thank you, Mamma" as she helps herself to what is forbidden—she makes me look at this world with a much less jaded view, revel in the beauty of each and every day, and want to bring the world to her—on a plate of course!!

MANEET AND DOUG ▶

When they say it takes a village to raise a child, that's true not only of children but also what this book has been—a child. I am so fortunate and thankful to have had so many talented people who were willing to work with me and bring this, my first book, to life.

foreword

A few years ago, in the progression of a long tasting menu, an Indian fine-dining chef in New York served us a tiny, delicious course of deep-fried cauliflower in a bright-red glaze. He then announced two things that our table of Midwesterners found intriguing.

One was that most modern versions of this dish, Gobi Manchurian, get much of their character from an ingredient you might not expect proper Indian chefs to highlight: ketchup. Also, the dish originated in China, a nation that shares (not always cordially) a 2,000-mile border with India, and whose émigrés to a small enclave in Calcutta had brought the treat with them and had adjusted it to local tastes. It's now [FOR CENTURIES, PERHAPS?] a hugely popular street food, often served on sticks, in cities from Mumbai to New Delhi, but especially in its adopted Calcutta home.

To many whose knowledge of Indian food is limited to naan and Chicken Tikka Masala, it might come as news that there are at least eighteen completely distinct cuisines in India, and that those cooking styles are as much a product of outside visitors, both of the friendly and marauder persuasion, as they are of local climate, class, religion, available produce, and geography. In short, much of Indian cooking is "fusion" cuisine.

My friend and *Chopped* colleague Maneet Chauhan has been working culinary mash-ups her whole career—ones that invited diners to precede that food with delightful, original cocktails. Now, in her newest chapter, the gorgeous *Flavors of My World*, Maneet herself becomes the friendly marauder, turning on its head the idea of the world's influences on Indian cooking to instead apply both her twist on Indian ideas and her classical CIA training to the very most unsuspecting of global cultures: Hungary, Japan, Greece, Ethiopia, even Ireland, which will surely be scandalized to learn she combines Guinness with Indian spices to produce a magnificent drink.

In these pages, photographed so beautifully by Quentin Bacon, she brings together the heavenly Gallic Pots de Crème, with a similar classic from Bengal, in Eastern India, Bhapa Doi, a roadside classic made from sweet, steamed yogurt. She puts her spin on the Kir Royale with the juice of Jamun berries, exclusive to the Indian subcontinent, and, of course, spices. She reboots Greek spanakopita by interpreting it with an eye to the Punjabi classic dish of spinach and paneer cheese with Sarson Saag Paneer Spanakopita, bringing mustard greens, fenugreek, and ginger to the phyllo party. She merges—of all things—Hungarian Goulash with a famous Hyderabad curry, Dalcha, a dish that long ago taught her the importance of freshly grinding your spices. Churros, the wonderful Mexican sticks of fried dough, are punched up with saffron and coconut milk to become Coconut Kesari.

And Mint Cilantro Shrimp Pakora Sushi—how could you read something that sounds so mind-blowingly delicious without flipping immediately to page 72?!

For newcomers to this land of beautiful spice, or those accustomed only to biryani and vindaloo, *Flavors of My World* lifts the veil of mystery on Indian cooking and shows how beautifully Indian flavors meld with those the world over in surprising and delicious ways. Her voice is clear, her stories, funny and personal, and—best of all—her directions are so simple that even beginners will soon find themselves whipping up feasts of fusion.

To that end, bon appétit! Or, should I say, Douzo meshiagare, Buen provechol, or Ăn ngon nhé? Doesn't matter how you say it. You're gonna love it.

—Ted Allen
Host, Food Network's *Chopped*
Brooklyn, 2013

my path to culinary enlightenment

Some say that I was born with a ladle in my hand. One thing's for certain, my passion for food started at an extremely early age. Some of my most cherished childhood memories were when I would join my father for our traditional Sunday outings to the farmer's market. We would scour the vast selection of colors, textures, aromas, and flavors—searching for the most beautiful and fresh produce, delicious meats, vibrant lentils, fragrant spices, and what seemed like an endless array of edible treats to bring home for the family dinner.

I was in love with the kitchen and I was always anxious to help my mom create these magnificent meals. I would perch myself on top of the counter, mesmerized, making sure that I wouldn't miss a thing as each and every ingredient was added to the pot or the pan. This curiosity and tireless interest persisted for years and ultimately developed into a fiery passion for cooking that never diminished—it escalated. It became more and more clear, every day, what my future would hold.

In the winter of 1998, my first introduction to the United States was when I arrived from India to attend the esteemed Culinary Institute of America. Initially touching down in Chicago to visit with my sister, I was astounded, as I had never experienced this type of culture, felt this intensity of cold, tasted these unusual foods, nor experienced this apparent obsession with world cuisine. It was certainly a shock to my system, but one that left me feeling extremely excited for what lay ahead.

For the better part of my 18 months at the CIA, I was the only Indian on campus—however, I felt extraordinarily connected because I was studying under the same roof as 2,000 other people whose lives also revolved around food—people who were as passionate as I was and had that requisite "little bit of crazy" that is necessary to make this their life. This was an environment in which I thrived and for the first time in my life, I was meeting people who had traveled the seven seas and had now come in search of the ultimate learning experience.

After a few months of studying, I decided it was time to introduce my new friends to the cuisine of my country, so off we went in search of an Indian restaurant in Hyde Park. Although I was very excited, let's just say this—I was shocked! This WAS NOT the food that I grew up with. Indian food is beautiful—it is varied—this was a shameful representation of our cuisine. How did this happen? Indian food is influenced by cultures from all over the world—the Spanish, the Portuguese, even French influences can be found in this exquisite cuisine. It became my mission to educate and find ways to reintroduce the foods of India with the respect they deserve.

Since my time at the CIA, I also have traveled extensively and it is these travels that have provided the inspiration for this book—these life experiences are highlighted and sometimes even defined by the extraordinary dishes that seem to somehow tell the story of a land and its people. The dining room, or kitchen, always seems to be the place where special times are marked—where families unite after a day of work, celebrate with friends on special occasions, or simply bond through the creation of a family meal. We as a people connect through our food; our cuisine tells a story and even marks the passage of time.

My time competing on Food Network's *Iron Chef* and becoming a judge on *Chopped* has given me valuable insight as to how people from different cultures and backgrounds experience food—how they adapt it to make it their own. The one thing that I have learned through my travels, both personal and those experienced vicariously through friends and family, is that eating an extraordinary meal can transport you to a different place and even a different time. So update your passport and join me on this culinary journey as we go off in search of the finest cuisine from 25 different countries. We will visit with people from near and far, experience their culture, and be guests at their tables. Then we will take inspiration from all of our travels and "bring it home" by putting our own twist on it—an Indian twist!

···ARGENTINA···

Argentinian people are well known for their passion for food. Needless to say, this is something with which I can completely relate.

Social gatherings in this beautiful country are commonly centered around sharing a meal, and an invitation to someone's home as a dinner guest is the most sincere gesture of friendship and warmth. The Sunday family dinner is widely considered to be the most significant meal of the week, and its highlights commonly include *asado* (barbecue).

It is quite common for the average Argentinian to eat four meals a day. It starts with *desayuno* (breakfast), then *almuerzo* (lunch). After work but before dinner, many Argentinians stop at cafés to drink espresso and eat *picadas* (appetizer-size portions of cheeses, meats, nuts and seafood). *Cena* (dinner) is the largest meal of the day and almost always includes meat—a prominent feature in Argentina's culinary landscape.

Argentinians have centuries of expertise in raising cattle and serving meat, which is why the country's steak houses are some of the best known in the world.

The most famous sauce adorning Argentinian beef is surely Argentina's shining star, chimichurri sauce. Traditionally made from parsley, garlic, olive oil, oregano, and vinegar, chimichurri allows for multitudes of variations from the minds of culinary artisans.

While "kebab" conjures images of individual pieces of meat and vegetables on a skewer cooked over an open flame, India's Seekh Kebab is different: spiced ground meat is shaped around a skewer.

These classic dishes finding a home together is surely a sign that cultures continue to meld and anything is possible with a bit of inspiration!

chimichurri seekh kebabs

Chimichurri

1 cup (packed) flat-leaf parsley
1/2 cup olive oil
1/3 cup red wine vinegar
1/4 cup (packed) cilantro
2 garlic cloves
3/4 teaspoon dried red pepper flakes
1/2 teaspoon ground cumin
1/2 teaspoon salt

Kebabs

2 1/2 pounds (1.25 kg) ground lamb
3/4 teaspoon garam masala
1 teaspoon minced garlic
2 tablespoons cashews, finely chopped
2 small red onions, finely chopped
2 tablespoons Indian black rock salt
1/2 teaspoon ground nutmeg
Sugarcane skewers
2 tablespoons butter, melted
1 teaspoon chaat masala to taste
Juice of 1 lemon

For the chimichurri, combine the parsley, olive oil, vinegar, cilantro, garlic, pepper flakes, cumin and salt in a food processor. Process until well blended. Let stand at least 1 hour for flavors to blend.

For the kebabs, combine 1/2 cup of the chimichurri, the lamb, garam masala, garlic, cashews, onions, rock salt and nutmeg. Knead the mixture to combine thoroughly. Form 1/3-cup portions of the mixture into kebabs around sugarcane skewers using wet hands.

Bake the kebabs at 400 degrees for about 8 minutes until nearly done to taste. Baste with the butter and bake until cooked through. Sprinkle with the chaat masala and lemon juice. Serve hot with the remaining chimichurri on the side. Makes 8 skewers.

chai yerba maté

Chai is a drink that is integral to an Indian household. When you wake up—chai. When guests arrive—chai. Tea time—chai. Before bed . . . you guessed it—chai!

One of my favorite memories is of riding the trains that traverse India and of the vendors weaving their way through the cars selling this beloved beverage. I can still hear the echo of their shouting, "Chai! Chai! Chai!"

The most memorable part of drinking chai on the train is that it is served in unglazed, earthen pots called *kulhars*. They impart a tremendously delicious, earthy taste that to this day I still try and re-create—a difficult task at best!

Yerba maté is a tea-like caffeinated infusion that in Argentina outsells coffee and tea combined. It's brewed and served in virtually every home and is a staple of their lifestyle. This cocktail, a blend of chai and yerba maté, combines some of my favorite flavors. Add vanilla-infused vodka, and you are in for a treat!

1/2 cup water
1 (1-inch) cinnamon stick
2 cardamom pods
2 whole cloves
1 (1/2-inch) piece ginger, crushed
1/3 cup milk
4 teaspoons sugar
1/2 teaspoon black tea leaves
2 yerba maté tea bags
2 ounces (60 ml) vanilla vodka

Combine the water, cinnamon, cardamom, cloves and ginger in a small saucepan. Bring to a boil. Simmer, covered, over low heat for 10 minutes. Add the milk and sugar. Return to a simmer. Add the tea leaves and yerba maté. Turn off the heat. Let stand 2 minutes, then strain and chill.

Fill a tall glass with ice. Add the vodka. Top with the chilled chai mixture.

15

···BRAZIL···

Each of Brazil's five geographic regions showcases unique cuisine that is distinctly different from the others, yet all are recognizably Brazilian. With a wide array of international influences including Amerindian, Portuguese, and borrowed styles from all over Europe, Asia, the Middle East, and Africa, Brazil's cuisine is diverse and exciting.

Some years back, my sister took a thrilling holiday in Brazil. Knowing that I would certainly want to hear all about the Brazilian cuisine, she told me about her favorite—delicious rice croquettes called *Bolinhos De Arrounces*. They sounded very much like Aloo Tikki, potato croquettes often served up by India's many street vendors.

Street food is very close to my heart. Growing up, these small carts and kiosks were in every nook and cranny. Due to my parents' concerns about the cleanliness of these culinary vendors, my sister and I were forbidden from eating street food. Being a culinary Magellan, my need to explore compelled me to coax my sister to sneak out of the house and try these delicious-looking dishes, which inspired this recipe.

bolinhos de arroz tikki

Filling
2/3 cup frozen green peas, thawed
1 1/2 teaspoons minced peeled fresh ginger
1/4 teaspoon chaat masala
1/4 teaspoon salt
Red chile powder to taste
1 teaspoon coarsely ground dry-roasted cumin seeds

Bolinhos
2 large potatoes, boiled
1 egg
1 red onion, finely chopped
1 serrano chile, seeded and minced
2 tablespoons chopped cilantro
1 garlic clove, minced
1 teaspoon salt
1/4 teaspoon pepper
1 tablespoon milk
1 cup cooked basmati rice
Oil for pan-frying
1 teaspoon chaat masala

With a wide array of international influences, Brazil's cuisine is diverse and exciting.

For the filling, mash the peas coarsely in a bowl with a spoon or fork. Add the ginger, masala, salt, chile and cumin and mix well.

For the bolinhos, peel the potatoes and mash them in a large bowl. Add the egg, onion, chile, cilantro, garlic, salt, pepper, milk and rice and mix well. Divide into ten portions. Form each portion into a ball. Flatten each into a 1/2-inch-thick patty. Place a small amount of the filling in the centers. Fold the patties to enclose the filling. Press the edges to seal. Gently flatten each into a 2-inch patty.

Pour enough oil into a nonstick pan to reach halfway up the side. Heat over low heat to 350 degrees. Add a few of the patties at a time. Pan-fry on both sides over very low heat until crisp golden brown, adding oil if needed. Sprinkle with the chaat masala. Makes 10 pieces.

jaggery tamarind caipirinha

The fermentation of sugarcane juice yields cachaça, the national spirit of Brazil and the key ingredient in the beloved caipirinha, a libation that is as versatile as it is delicious. Referred to as "fire water," cachaça is a liquor so potent that some Brazilians even run their cars on it—really!

In my youth I had a passion for climbing the tamarind tree in my neighbor's backyard. I scaled its branches, plucked the tasty morsels, and would make the "sour puss face" at the fruit's natural tartness. This flavor, always fresh in my mind, pairs exquisitely with the bold flavor of the Brazilian sugarcane liquor and jaggery, a coarse, unrefined sugar made from sugarcane juice, and will hopefully awaken your passion too.

2 tablespoons jaggery or gur
1/2 teaspoon crushed black peppercorns
1/2 teaspoon tamarind concentrate
1 lime wedge
2 ounces (60 ml) cachaça or white rum
Club soda

Crush the sugar, peppercorns, tamarind and lime in the bottom of a glass. Add ice cubes. Add cachaça and stir to blend. Finish with a dash of club soda.

···CHILE···

Curanto, meaning "hot stones," is a time-tested and customary Chilean method of cooking seafood and meat. Similar to a traditional clambake, layers of chicken, seafood, sausages, pork, and vegetables are arranged in a pit filled with red-hot stones. Each layer is then covered with nalca leaves (similar to rhubarb), which provide additional moisture and seal in the steam. The flavors of the meat and seafood dance together along with a subtle woodsy flavor provided by the nalca leaves, delivering a timeless dish which has been celebrated and enjoyed for thousands of years.

A home version called *pulmay* features the same ingredients, but is cooked in a pot. I've replaced the nalca leaves with savoy cabbage. It's the perfect meal for entertaining a crowd, and this recipe incorporates a little from both methods, as well as my own personal twist—one that was inspired by my time studying hotel management near Malabar in the southwestern coast of India in Northern Kerala.

This important port town was a stop for traders on the ancient Spice Route. Consequently, Malabari cuisine, which features coconut, coriander, and cinnamon, was also heavily influenced by the Arab, Portuguese, Chinese, and even Italian culinary arts.

chilean malabari "curanto"

Chicken and Marinade

1/2 cup frozen coconut

1 (1-inch) piece fresh turmeric root

5 whole red chiles

1 tablespoon coriander seeds

1 tablespoon cumin seeds

1 (1-inch) ginger

1 (1-inch) cinnamon stick

4 garlic cloves

Salt to taste

11/2 pounds (3/4 kg) skinless boneless
    chicken thighs, cut into 1-inch cubes

Curanto

2 tablespoons olive oil

11/2 pounds (3/4 kg) mini Yukon Gold
    potatoes, quartered lengthwise

1 red bell pepper, cut into 1/2-inch slices

1 Spanish onion, sliced

1 banana pepper, thickly sliced

2 tablespoons chopped garlic

Salt and pepper to taste

1 large savoy cabbage, leaves removed
    from core

1 cup (1/2-inch) slices Spanish chorizo

3 pounds (1.5 kg) clams

2 pounds (1 kg) mussels, scrubbed

1 cup coconut milk

For the chicken, grind or pound the coconut, turmeric, chiles, coriander, cumin, ginger, cinnamon, garlic and salt to a paste. Combine with the chicken in a large bowl. Marinate for at least 2 hours.

For the curanto, heat the olive oil in a large grill-proof soup pot or Dutch oven over high heat. Sauté the chicken until lightly browned. Add the potatoes, bell pepper, onion, banana pepper and half the garlic. Season with salt and pepper. Cook for 4 minutes until the vegetables are softened. Preheat the oven to 325 degrees.

Cover the top with about one-third of the cabbage leaves. Add the sausage in a layer and cover with more cabbage leaves. Add the clams, mussels and remaining garlic. Pour the coconut milk over the top. Add a final layer of cabbage leaves. Cover the pot. Bake for 40 minutes. Serve hot. Makes 8 servings.

Curanto,
a time-
tested and
customary
Chilean
method of
cooking
seafood
and meat,
produces
a timeless
dish which
has been
celebrated
and enjoyed
for thousands
of years.

curried cazuela en champagne

Bellini-like Cazuela en Champagne, blended with Indian spice and fruit, delivers a taste sensation that will keep your guests on their toes. It's delicious alongside Sunday brunch, or can comfortably stand on its own at a cocktail party. Trade out the Champagne for sparkling apple juice for a delicious non-alcoholic alternative.

2 ounces (60 ml) ripe mango
1 tablespoon confectioners' sugar
1/2 teaspoon lime juice
1/2 teaspoon Madras curry powder
4 ounces (120 ml) chilled Champagne or
    sparkling wine
1 teaspoon fresh pomegranate seeds

Purèe the mango, confectioners' sugar and lime juice in a blender. Stir in the curry powder. Chill. Pour the mixture into a Champagne flute. Top with Champagne. Garnish with pomegranate seeds and serve at once.

···CHINA···

At age three or four, my passion for food was already apparent as the soaring popularity of Chinese food in India spawned some extremely popular commercial products. My favorite was Maggi Noodles, which are very similar to America's instant ramen noodles. At that time, a lot of the fine dining restaurants in India were Chinese. I clearly remember my grandparents taking the whole family out for a very special dinner. As the server approached with a beautiful platter of lo mein, much to the embarrassment of my family, I squealed and yelled out, "Maggi noodles!"

These iconic commercial items, much to the dismay of epicureans worldwide, are perceived as dietary staples of these countries. But Maggi Noodles are about as Chinese as Spaghetti-O's are Italian. Still, they're a guilty pleasure to many closeted junk-food-junkies.

As one of the original fusion cuisines, Chinese food is fused with local tastes so that dishes experienced in different places will be just that—different. The Chinese cuisine served in India, Peru, and the United States will not necessarily have a tremendous amount in common. However, its influence has certainly found its place in the cuisines of many cultures.

Recently, I competed in a Chinese cooking competition that was broadcast internationally live from Times Square in New York City. The sheer ethnic display of this event, the flaming woks, and the gaze of the huge crowd not only inspired me, but drove me to delve further into this compelling cuisine. I and a host of other "celebrity" chefs were challenged to make a traditional version of a Chinese staple, Kung Pao Chicken, within a very short time frame—a pressure cooker indeed! As much as I enjoyed the process and ultimately the dish, I craved the addition of a couple of Indian spices. Indo-Chinese is enjoyed by many Indians, and I hope you enjoy one of my favorites of this genre.

indian-style chile chicken

Chicken
2 pounds (1 kg) boneless chicken thighs,
    cut into 1-inch cubes
1/4 teaspoon red chili powder
1/2 teaspoon white pepper
1 tablespoon soy sauce
2 teaspoons vinegar
1 tablespoon ketchup
1 teaspoon ginger-garlic paste
Salt to taste
1 tablespoon cornstarch
1 egg
Oil for deep-frying

Vegetables and sauce
1 tablespoon vegetable oil
2 small red onions, sliced
2 green onions, chopped
1 (1/2-inch) piece ginger, thinly sliced
3 garlic cloves, chopped
5 or 6 serrano chiles, chopped
1 green bell pepper, cut lengthwise into
    1/4-inch slices
2 cups chicken broth or water
1 teaspoon sugar
1/4 teaspoon red chili powder
Salt and white pepper to taste
1 tablespoon soy sauce
1 tablespoon ketchup
1 tablespoon cornstarch
Chopped green onion tops, for garnish

One of the original fusion cuisines, Chinese food is fused with local tastes.

For the chicken, combine the chicken, red chili powder, white pepper, soy sauce, vinegar, ketchup, garlic-ginger paste and salt in a bowl and mix well. Let stand 10 to 15 minutes. Add the cornstarch and egg and mix well. Heat oil in a large skillet or deep-fryer to 325 degrees. Fry the chicken until golden brown.

For the vegetables and sauce, heat the oil in a skillet or wok over medium-high heat. Add the onions, ginger, garlic, chiles and bell pepper. Sauté for a few seconds. Add the broth and bring to a boil. Add the sugar, red chili powder, salt, white pepper, soy sauce and ketchup and mix well. Add the fried chicken. Cook, stirring, until chicken is coated with the sauce.

Combine the cornstarch with 1/2 cup water and mix well. Add to the sauce, stirring constantly to prevent lumps. Cook for 2 to 3 minutes. Serve hot, garnished with green onion tops. Makes 4 servings.

kumquat chile cocktail

When Americans think of Chinese cocktails, it is often the iconic drink umbrella that springs to mind. The truth about the origins of the drink umbrella is still somewhat murky. However, contrary to popular belief, the shade provided by a cocktail umbrella is of secondary importance to its aesthetic qualities.

Kumquat is a favorite in Chinese cocktails and rightfully so, as its diverse sweetness lends itself as a good partner to many liquors. As you will see and hopefully taste, when married to the spiciness of the chili pepper, magic appears and the cocktail vanishes.

3 kumquats
1/4 small red chile, seeded
3 mint leaves
2 ounces (60 ml) white rum
1 ounce (30 ml) simple syrup
1 teaspoon grenadine
Lime soda
2 whole small red Thai or bird chiles
   for garnish

Muddle the kumquats, 1/4 chile, mint, rum and simple syrup in a cocktail shaker. Add the grenadine and top with ice. Cover and shake a few times. Pour into 2 short glasses. Top with soda.

Make a small cut in the side of each whole chile. Perch them on the rims of the glasses. Serve immediately.

···CUBA···

Ropa vieja, loosely translated, means "old clothes." Though the Cubans refer to it as their own, this dish originated in the Canary Islands, where boats traveling back and forth to America would make a stop. With continuous immigration to Cuba and the Caribbean, *ropa vieja* inevitably arrived in the islands. In much the same way that Cubans have put a unique twist on African rhythms, they have also adopted *ropa vieja* and added a little Cuban panache.

There are many theories as to how this dish was named. One of the more popular folklore tales describes a man whose family was coming to visit his home for dinner. Being very poor, he could not purchase enough food to provide a meal, so to remedy his situation, he went to his closet, gathered some old clothes and imbued them with his love. Upon cooking them in a stew pot, his deep love for his family turned them into a wonderful beef stew.

This delightful culinary expression is commonly cooked for a family meal and is enjoyed at many a holiday. *Rogan josh*, the fused element of this dish, is an aromatic lamb dish of Persian origin and a signature recipe of Kashmiri cuisine. These two were a natural fit and one that I am sure will deliver delicious results for you and your family!

ropa vieja rogan josh

2 pounds (1 kg) boneless goat,
   cut into cubes
1/2 cup plain yogurt
1/4 cup garlic-ginger paste
Salt to taste
1 cup roughly chopped bacon
1 (2-inch) cinnamon stick
5 or 6 whole green cardamom pods
8 to 10 whole cloves
2 bay leaves
1 teaspoon peppercorns
1 medium yellow onion, thinly sliced
1 red bell pepper, thinly sliced

1 green pepper, thinly sliced
1 yellow bell pepper, thinly sliced
1/2 cup tomato paste
1 tablespoon dried thyme
1 tablespoon dried oregano
1/4 teaspoon ground turmeric
1/2 teaspoon paprika
2 teaspoons garam masala
2 cups chicken stock
1/2 cup halved pitted green olives
3 tablespoons capers, rinsed
   and drained
1/4 cup roughly chopped cilantro

Combine the goat, yogurt, garlic-ginger paste and salt in a bowl and mix well.

Cook the bacon in a 6-quart Dutch oven over medium-high heat until the fat melts. Add the cinnamon stick, cardamom, cloves, bay leaves and peppercorns. Sauté briefly. Add the onion and bell peppers and sauté until they are light golden. Add the goat mixture and sauté briefly. Add the tomato paste, thyme, oregano, turmeric, paprika and garam masala. Cook until the oil separates from the mixture at the edge.

Add the chicken stock. Reduce the heat to medium low. Cook, covered, for 2 to 3 hours until the meat is very tender. Remove the meat from the stew and shred it. Return to the pan, along with the olives and capers. Cook, uncovered, for about 30 minutes or until the liquid in the pan thickens. Add the cilantro just before serving. Makes 4 servings.

masala coke cuba libre

The exact origin of the Cuba Libre is one of mystery and has been argued by many. One point that is agreed on is the timing: the Cuba Libre seems to have first been sipped in 1900, the year Coca-Cola arrived in Cuba. While the beverage is thought to be first introduced to the island by American troops, "Cuba Libre!" was the battle cry of the Cuba Liberation Army during the war of independence that ended in 1898.

Since spice and masala go into everything in India, why should Coca-Cola be exempt? In India, Masala Coke has been all the rage for many years!

One of my favorite authors, Suketu Mehta, best describes the Masala Coke in his book, *Maximum city: Bombay Lost and Found,* as follows:

"When the Coke is poured into the glass, which has a couple of teaspoons of the masala waiting to attack the liquid from the bottom up, the American drink froths up in astonished anger. The waiter stands at your booth, waiting until the froth dies down, then puts in a little more of the Coke, then waits a moment more, then pours in the rest. And, lo! it has become a Hindu Coke. The alien invader has come into the country. It has been accepted into the pantheon of local drinks but has a little spice added to it, a little more zing. The cocaine is back in the Coke."

One thing's for certain, this spicy twist will get your mouth's attention!

Juice of 1/2 lime
1/2 teaspoon chaat masala
Black salt to taste
1/4 teaspoon white pepper
1/4 teaspoon crumbled dried mint
Coca-Cola
2 ounces (60 ml) Cuban rum

Combine the lime juice, masala, black salt and white pepper in a tall glass. Add the cola, a little at a time, stirring continuously to allow the soda to froth up, until the glass is full. Crush the mint leaves slightly and add to the glass. Add the rum.

···ENGLAND···

What is it about England that completely fascinates me? Maybe it's the lords and ladies, or the Enid Blyton books that I grew up reading. It could be the romance of the Colonial times—to me England is simply a country that I love. Even my husband jokes with me that I married him because he went to the University of Bournemouth and therefore has a bit of English in him.

The British adore Indian food. Chicken Tikka Masala is widely considered England's "national dish," and is probably one of the earliest food fusions. Samosas are available at the corner newsstand, and even a world-famous store like Harrods offers a Chicken Tikka sandwich.

I wanted to do my own exploration of Indian flavors in an English dish, so I took a run at the famous fish and chips!

Winston Churchill called them "the good companions," and John Lennon smothered his in ketchup. This flagship dish of England has spread to restaurants and bars worldwide. For generations, this perfect pub-inspired meal has fed millions of memories and greased the eager fingers of diners enjoying a hearty plateful. I particularly enjoy this slight twist and am confident that you will as well.

amritsari fish and masala aloo chips

Fish and Marinade
1/4 cup malt vinegar
1 teaspoon grated ginger
1 teaspoon pepper
1/2 teaspoon ajwain
1 teaspoon salt
2 pounds (1 kg) skinless Alaskan cod, cut into medium chunks

Batter
1 cup besan (chick-pea flour)
1/2 cup rice flour
1 teaspoon ginger paste
2 teaspoons garlic paste
1/2 teaspoon ajwain
1 teaspoon chili powder
2 tablespoons kasoori methi
1 teaspoon baking powder
Salt to taste
Ice water
Vegetable oil for frying
Malt vinegar

Enjoy my own exploration of Indian flavors in an English dish —a perfect pub-inspired meal which has fed millions of memories.

For the marinade, combine the vinegar, ginger, pepper, ajwain and salt in a bowl and mix well. Add the fish. Marinate for 30 minutes. Remove the fish from the marinade and pat dry.

For the batter, combine besan, rice flour, ginger paste, garlic paste, ajwain, chili powder, kasoori methi, baking powder and salt in a bowl. Stir in ice water until the consistency of pancake batter. Coat the fish with batter. Let stand for 15 minutes. Heat oil in a large skillet to 360 degrees. Fry the fish until golden brown. Serve hot with malt vinegar, salt and Masala Aloo Chips (recipe follows). Makes 6 servings.

masala aloo chips

Masala Aloo
1/2 teaspoon ground cumin
1/2 teaspoon ground ginger
5 dried whole red chiles
1 tablespoon amchur
1/2 teaspoon coarse salt

Chips
4 medium potatoes
Salt to taste
Vegetable oil for deep-frying

For the masala, toast the cumin in a small skillet over medium-high heat until fragrant. (You can use whole cumin seeds if you prefer.) Combine the cumin, ginger, chiles, amchur and salt in a spice grinder or blender. Process to a powder.

For the chips, slice the potatoes paper-thin into a bowl of cold water. Drain and rinse, then refill the bowl with water. Add the salt and potatoes. Let stand for 30 minutes. Drain, rinse and drain again.

Heat oil in a deep-fryer to 365 degrees. Fry the potatoes in small batches until golden. Remove them immediately as they turn golden. Drain on paper towels. Season with the masala aloo.

indian summer pimm's

First produced in 1823 as an afternoon refreshment, gin-based, spicy-sweet Pimm's is a staple of English culture. This British beverage is almost as much a tradition as the cup of tea, and its loyal followers have introduced it around the world. Closely associated with culture and high society, this is one beverage that has re-emerged to great acclaim and challenged the mightiest of mixologists to elevate it to an even higher level. So with great admiration and respect, I throw my hat in the ring!

1 lemon, sliced into half-moons
1 mango slice
1 star fruit slice
2 English or Persian cucumber slices
3 large mint sprigs and several additional mint leaves, gently crushed
1/2 teaspoon amchur
3 ounces (90 ml) Pimm's No. 1
Lemon-lime soda

Fill a glass with ice. Add the lemon, mango, star fruit, cucumber and mint. Sprinkle with the amchur. Add the Pimm's and top with soda.

···ETHIOPIA···

I strongly recollect the first time I ever tasted Ethiopian food. I had just arrived in the United States to start my education at the Culinary Institute of America (CIA) in Hyde Park, New York. First, though, I took a slight detour to Chicago to visit my sister. Besides experiencing the chilling cold for the first time, I had the opportunity to try any number of global cuisines—ones that I had never even thought about! One of these was Ethiopian, at an amazing restaurant where I enjoyed *Doro Wat*, Ethiopia's best-known dish, for the first time.

What first struck me was that the flavors were so distinct, yet so familiar. A traditional doro wat uses *niter kibbeh*, a seasoned, clarified butter common in Ethiopian cooking. Its preparation is very similar to that of ghee, which is predominant in Indian food. The difference is that niter kebbeh is simmered with spices such as cumin, coriander, turmeric, cardamom, cinnamon, or nutmeg before straining. This imparts a distinct and spicy flavor profile, and although the technique is different, the flavor combination is very reminiscent of Indian cuisine.

I received my bachelor's in hotel management at a school in Manipal. As Mangalore was the closest "big town," my friends and I would visit often, and being students on a budget, we ate at the many roadside shacks along the way. These dishes, though simple and rustic, had a complexity of flavors that many accomplished chefs to this day strive to achieve.

The similar spicing of doro wat and the food of Mangalore gave me the idea of adding traditional Mangaloran coconut and curry leaves to it as an exotic addition.

mangalorean doro wat

2 pounds (3/4 kg) skinless chicken legs
   and thighs, cut into 1-inch pieces
Juice of 1 lemon
Salt to taste
1 medium onion, coarsely chopped
5 garlic cloves, minced
1 (1-inch) piece ginger, sliced
1 tablespoon ghee
6 whole green cardamom pods
2 teaspoons cumin seeds
4 to 6 dried red Kashmiri chiles

1 cinnamon stick
6 whole cloves
1/2 cup frozen grated coconut
1 teaspoon tamarind paste
1 tablespoon ghee
2 tablespoons paprika
5 to 8 curry leaves
1 tomato, finely chopped
Cayenne pepper to taste
Black pepper to taste
4 hard-boiled eggs

Combine the chicken, lemon juice and salt in a large non-reactive bowl. Marinate for 30 minutes.

Purée the onion, garlic and ginger in a food processor or blender, adding a little water if needed.

Heat 1 tablespoon ghee in a small pan. Add the cardamom, cumin, chiles, cinnamon, cloves and coconut and fry for 2 minutes. Let cool. Add the tamarind and about 3/4 cup to 1 cup water or chicken stock. Grind the mixture to a smooth paste in a blender or food processor.

Heat 1 tablespoon ghee in a skillet. Add the paprika and mix well until the butter is colored. Cook for 1 minute, watching carefully so it doesn't burn. Add the curry leaves and puréed mixture. Cook for 5 to 10 minutes until the moisture evaporates and the onion cooks down and loses its raw aroma.

Add the cardamom-coconut paste, chicken and tomato. Season with the cayenne pepper, salt and black pepper. Bring to a boil. Reduce the heat to low and simmer, covered, for 15 to 20 minutes, adding water as needed to maintain a sauce consistency. Add the eggs. Cook for 5 to 10 minutes longer, until the chicken is cooked through and very tender. Makes 4 servings.

Distinct, yet so familiar, the flavor combination in this dish is very reminiscent of Indian cuisine.

darjeeling tea tej

Tej (Ethiopian honey wine) is a widely consumed favorite and is flavored with the powdered leaves and twigs of gesho, a hops-like ingredient that adds a slight bitterness. Commonly homemade, tej is also widely available in Ethiopian bars called *tej betoch*. Tej has a deceptively sweet taste that can mask its high alcohol content, which varies greatly according to the length of fermentation, so proceed with playful caution. This recipe's addition of star anise and darjeeling tea adds a lovely level of sophistication and worldly spice.

2 cups water
2 tablespoons Darjeeling tea leaves
4 star anise
1/3 cup honey
1 (750-ml) bottle white wine
Star anise, for garnish

Heat the water, tea, 4 star anise and the honey in a small saucepan over low heat, stirring until well combined. Chill.

Strain the tea mixture. Combine with the wine in a decorative glass decanter and mix well. Serve lightly chilled. Garnish each serving with 1 star anise.

···FRANCE···

Pots de Crème is a lightly set, baked custard and has been a celebrated dessert for hundreds of years. The French do not have a word for "custard," and subsequently the dish is simply referred to as "crème." The "pots" that this delectable treat are served in are typically made of porcelain, hold approximately 3 ounces of custard, and are commonly referred to as "petits pots." The first time I had the pleasure of tasting pots de crème was when I was attending CIA. I had never tried this incredibly delicious and creamy concoction, but the cooking style closely resembled *bhapa doi,* which is certainly India's answer to this classic, sugary French custard.

Bhapa Doi is a steamed, flavored, sweet yogurt dish that is made especially during Durga Puja festival, which is an annual occurrence and takes place in Bengal, in the Eastern part of India. At times, *bhapa doi* can be found roadside, like so many of the world's culinary treasures, and is consumed *en masse* with happy faces. Joining these two similar desserts, seemed like a natural union, and I am excited to share just what my experimentation has uncovered.

pa doi pots de crème

2 cups heavy cream
2 vanilla beans
6 egg yolks
$1/2$ cup sugar
$1/2$ cup sweetened condensed milk
1 cup plain Greek yogurt
$1/2$ teaspoon ground green cardamom
Fresh pomegranate seeds, for garnish
Finely sliced pistachios, for garnish

India's answer to the classic, sugary French custard.

Pour the cream into small saucepan. Split the vanilla beans into halves lengthwise and scrape the seeds into the cream. Add the pods. Heat the cream until it steams. Cover the pan, turn off the heat, and let stand for 10 to 15 minutes. Remove the pods.

Preheat the oven to 300 degrees. Beat the egg yolks and sugar in a bowl until light in color. Stir in about one-fourth of the cream. Pour all of the egg yolk mixture into the cream in the saucepan and mix well.

Combine the condensed milk, yogurt and cardamom in a bowl. Fold into the egg mixture.

Divide the custard among 12 (4-ounce) ramekins. Set the ramekins in a baking dish. Add enough water to the baking dish to reach halfway up the sides of the ramekins. Cover the pan with foil.

Bake for 30 to 40 minutes until the centers are barely set. Chill in the refrigerator. Garnish with pomegranate seeds and pistachios to serve. Makes 12 (4-ounce) servings.

jamun kir royale

Kir originated in Burgundy, France, and is named after the priest Canon Félix Kir. A hero in the French Resistance during the Second World War, as well as the mayor of the Burgundian town of Dijon from 1945 to 1968, he was much revered and a proponent of local products. He created this beloved drink by mixing the local white wine made from the bone-dry Aligoté grape with the local black currant liqueur, crème de cassis. The combination was such a colossal hit that it became famous worldwide, where it was often adapted to include other regional wines and liqueurs. Kir royale differs from kir in that it is made using Champagne rather than the Aligoté white wine.

Jamuns are absolutely delicious berries exclusive to the Indian sub-continent. They look like large black olives and are ripe for the picking in India's summertime. As the monsoon season provides much-awaited relief from the scorching Indian summer, the winds provide a shower of ripe jamuns falling from the trees. Jamuns amped up with a touch of chaat masala and chili was commonly sold by roadside vendors. As children, we enjoyed the deliciously tart, sweet and spicy concoction, which had the fun side effect of coloring our tongues blue. While this interpretation of the Kir Royale will not turn your tongue blue, it will certainly be something deliciously different for your mouth!

1 ounce (30 ml) crème de cassis
1 ounce (30 ml) jamun juice
1/2 teaspoon chaat masala
3 ounces (90 ml) chilled Champagne
Lemon twist, for garnish

Combine the crème de cassis, jamun juice and chaat masala in a champagne flute. Top with the Champagne. Garnish with a lemon twist.

···GREECE···

A beautiful country of breathtaking views and an astounding history, Greece has a tendency to heighten all of the senses. Perhaps the single most inspiring thing about Greek cuisine is that sharing a meal with others is as important as the food itself. Greeks even have a special word for this—*parea*, a transcendence of the dinner table to include the overall spirit of your surroundings. What a beautiful word to embody special times.

While the primary ingredients of Greek cooking are not extensive (olive oil, honey, yogurt, fresh fruits and vegetables, lamb, and fish), the manner in which they are prepared seems to have endless variations and tastes. One bonus aspect of this elegant cuisine is that whether you eat meat or are vegetarian, it is arguably the healthiest diet on the planet.

In Punjab, the acumen of a cook is commonly measured by his or her expertise in creating the quintessential *sarson saag*. It is a staple in any Punjabi household, and each and every auntie in our colony had her own secret recipe for making the perfect sarson saag. It included a combination of greens, an array of spices, and at times, even a secret ingredient slipped into the dish when nobody was looking. I seriously think that my mom's magic for a delicious sarson saag was slow cooking with lots and lots of freshly homemade butter—and of course a healthy dose of love. The fusion of this Indian classic with classic Greek spanakopita is a match made in heaven.

sarson saag paneer spanakopita

1 pound (¹/2 kg) spinach, finely chopped
1 pound (¹/2 kg) mustard greens,
    finely chopped
8 ounces (¹/4 kg) frozen fenugreek
    leaves (kasoori methi)
2 serrano chiles, thinly sliced
Salt to taste
1 tablespoon besan (chick-pea flour)
    or cornmeal
2 to 3 tablespoons ghee

1 large onion, chopped
1 tablespoon grated ginger
1 tablespoon grated garlic
1 teaspoon garam masala
1 cup grated paneer (Indian fresh
    cheese), or 8 ounces, diced
1 cup ricotta or cottage cheese
¹/4 cup melted butter
¹/4 cup olive oil
1 pound (¹/2 kg) phyllo pastry sheets

Combine the spinach, mustard greens, fenugreek leaves, chiles and salt in a soup pan.
Add 1 cup water and bring to a boil. Cover and cook until tender. Drain the liquid, then
squeeze out excess moisture. Purée the greens to form a coarse paste.

Toast the besan in a dry skillet until the raw smell is gone.

Heat the ghee in a skillet over medium heat and sauté the onion until pale golden. Add
the besan, ginger and garlic and mix well. Let cool.

Combine the paneer and ricotta cheese in a large bowl. Add the cooled greens and mix
well. Combine the melted butter and olive oil in a bowl. Oil a 9x12-inch pan with a little
of the butter mixture.

Preheat the oven to 350 degrees. Remove the phyllo from the plastic sleeve. Most phyllo
is cut into 12x18-inch sheets. Unroll the sheets. Use scissors or a sharp knife to cut the
sheets into halves to make two 9x12-inch sheets. Cover one stack with waxed paper and
a damp paper towel to prevent it from drying out.

Layer 10 sheets of the phyllo on the bottom of the pan, brushing each sheet with the
butter mixture. Spoon the spinach mixture onto the phyllo and press into an even layer
with a spatula.

Layer another 10 sheets over the filling, brushing each sheet with the butter mixture.

Score the top of the phyllo to simplify cutting later. Bake for 20 to 25 minutes until deep
golden brown. Makes 10 servings.

The fusion
of an Indian
classic with
the classic
Greek
spanakopita
is a match
made in
heaven.

spicy coconut ouzo

Ouzo has its roots in *tsipouro* (brandy), which is said to have been the pet project of a group of fourteenth-century monks living in a monastery on Mount Athos. It is certainly the quintessential Greek liquor and widely consumed there. Some are purists and will only drink it straight, but it lends itself to many possibilities when it comes to the art of mixology.

When I first tried ouzo, I was visiting my sister and brother-in-law who had "discovered" this amazing liquor. That evening, between the three of us, we managed to finish the entire bottle! Create your own cross-cultural adventure with this Greek-inspired drink.

2 ounces (60 ml) coconut milk
1/2 teaspoon thinly sliced peeled ginger
2 slices serrano chile with seeds
1 teaspoon sugar
3 tablespoons lime juice
1 ounce (30 ml) ouzo
2 ounces coconut water
Roasted coconut flakes, for garnish

Muddle the coconut milk, ginger and chile in a tall, thin glass. Add the sugar and lime juice and mix well. Fill the glass with ice. Add the ouzo and stir to combine. Add the coconut water. Garnish with coconut flakes.

···HUNGARY···

Hungarian goulash (*gulyás*) is neither a soup nor a stew—it's a delicious dish in its own category and Hungary's most famous culinary expression. There is still much confusion and misconception surrounding its exact preparation method, and even in Hungary seemingly every other housewife has her own recipe, adding or omitting certain ingredients, maintaining that her *gulyás* is the most authentic!

Gulyás, Magyar for "herdsman," became a national dish in the late 1800s. A filling and hearty stew commonly prepared with beef, lamb or pork, vegetables, and spices, goulash gets its flavor from slow-cooking these richly flavored cuts of meat and, of course, the addition of paprika.

Dalcha is a famous curry in Hyderabad, combining mutton and *channa dal*, and is the perfect bridge to this classic Hungarian masterpiece. When I was involved in my first externship at the prestigious Meridian Hotel in New Delhi India, I learned the secret of a good *dalcha*. My teachers, who were all extremely well-educated chefs, all seemed to come from generation after generation of cooks who would pass down valuable knowledge and wisdom. They taught me that the use of freshly ground spices in this dish was critical. Now with many more years of experience under my belt, I concur!

dalcha hungarian goulash

1/2 cup split chick-peas (channa dal)
2 tablespoons all-purpose flour
Salt and black pepper to taste
1 pound (1/2 kg) lamb stew meat, cut into 1-inch cubes
4 tablespoons olive oil
2 red onions, sliced
3 tomatoes, chopped
1 sprig of fresh rosemary
4 teaspoons minced garlic
4 teaspoons grated ginger
1 tablespoon freshly ground coriander
1/2 teaspoon sweet paprika
1/2 teaspoon smoked paprika
1/8 to 1/4 teaspoon cayenne pepper
1 teaspoon ground turmeric
1 1/2 cups chopped carrots
2 sweet potatoes, peeled and cut into a 1-inch cubes
Juice of 1 lime

Neither a soup nor a stew, Hungary's most famous culinary expression is a delicious dish in its own category.

Rinse the chick-peas and soak in cold water in a bowl for 30 minutes; drain and set aside.

Combine the flour, salt and black pepper on a large plate. Add the lamb and toss to coat. Heat 2 tablespoons of the olive oil in a large saucepan and fry the lamb for 3 minutes on each side until browned. Set aside. Cook the onions in the pan drippings until golden-brown. Set aside.

Heat the remaining olive oil in the saucepan. Add the tomatoes and rosemary and stir to coat. Add the lamb, onions, garlic, ginger, coriander, sweet paprika, smoked paprika, cayenne pepper, turmeric, salt and pepper and mix well. Add the carrots, sweet potatoes, chick-peas and 3 cups water and mix well.

Reduce the heat to medium-low. Partially cover the pan. Simmer until the lamb is very tender and the chick-peas have broken down to form a rich sauce, adding water if needed. Remove from the heat. Stir in the lime juice and season to taste. Makes 6 servings.

bollywood cherry pálinka

Pálinka is a broad term for an alcoholic drink distilled from any fruit grown on Hungarian soil. It is commonly distilled in rural areas with greatly varying degrees of quality. This has made sipping a glass of pálinka something that attracts the connoisseur, as the sheer variety of what is available is staggering. One of the obvious signs of quality, which that doesn't take a connoisseur to recognize, is the lack of a hangover the following morning.

As with Champagne, strict laws imposed by the EU outline what can and can't be called pálinka. This protects the name and ultimately helps guarantee a quality product. A dash of Indian spice adds a spirited twist to the following cocktail and is sure to have you breaking into a Bollywood dance number, so enjoy!

1/4 cup pitted dark cherries
1/4 teaspoon garam masala
1/2 ounce (15 ml) vanilla-infused
   simple syrup
1 ounce (30 ml) gypsy cherry pálinka
1/2 ounce (15 ml) amaretto
4 ounces (120 ml) brut Champagne
Cherry, for garnish

Muddle the pitted cherries, garam masala and simple syrup in a shaker. Add the cherry palinka and amaretto. Add ice, cover, and shake to blend. Strain into a Champagne flute. Top with Champagne. Garnish with a cherry.

···INDONESIA···

Early on in my relationship with my husband, he lived in Indonesia for business. During our many phone calls (which cost enough to put a down payment on a house), he would describe the incredible *nasi goring*, or fried rice, a national dish full of bold flavors.

A few years ago I was invited to Southeast Asia to cook in Jakarta. I had heard quite a bit about Jakarta's food—the freshness of the produce, the amazing markets, and of course, *nasi goring*. It was the first thing I tried. The flavor profiles of Indonesian cuisine were truly inspiring and a logical fit with one of my Indian favorites, *panch puran*.

Traditionally, *panch puran* is a mixture of five spices in equal proportion, including fenugreek, black mustard seeds, cumin seeds, onion seeds, and fennel seeds. However, lovers of this spice blend vary the proportions to suit their personal palates.

A delicious union of soulmates, this blend of flavors will create epicurean memories that will keep you coming back.

panch puran nasi goreng

1 egg, lightly beaten
2 tablespoons (or more) vegetable oil
1 tablespoon panch puran spice mix (equal parts mustard seeds, fennel seeds,
    cumin seeds, fenugreek seeds and onion seeds)
5 shallots, sliced
2 garlic cloves, sliced
3 red chiles, sliced
1 teaspoon dried shrimp paste
1 cup shredded cabbage
1 cup chopped deveined shrimp or sliced chicken
4 cups cold cooked rice
1/2 teaspoon salt
1 tablespoon sweet soy sauce
Cucumber slices, for garnish
Tomato slices, for garnish
6 fried eggs, for garnish

The flavor profiles of Indonesian cuisine were truly inspiring in this delicious union of soul mates.

Cook the beaten egg in a small amount of oil in a wok. Remove the egg to a plate to cool. Shred the egg using a fork.

Heat the oil in a wok. Add the spice mix. Sauté until the spices start to crackle. Add the shallots, garlic, chiles and shrimp paste. Sauté until the shallots are tender. Add the cabbage and shrimp. Cook until shrimp are cooked through.

Raise the heat to high. Fluff the rice with a fork and add it to the wok, along with the salt and soy sauce. Add additional oil if needed. Stir-fry until well mixed and heated through.

Garnish each serving with cucumber, tomato, some of the shredded egg and a fried egg. Makes 6 servings.

garam masala alpukat

Initially the thought of avocado in your coffee drink may make you grimace, but one sip of this cocktail based on the classic Indonesian delight will change your mind forever. *Alpukat*, a surprisingly delicious and refreshing Indonesian coffee drink, gets its richness and body from yes, avocado. In Indonesia, it is commonly served over ice, but with the addition of a bit of spice and alcohol, we prefer the ice blended right in, milkshake-style!

1 ripe avocado
3 tablespoons sweetened condensed
  milk
1 cup (about) milk
3 tablespoons chocolate syrup
1 tablespoon garam masala
1 ounce (30 ml) coffee liqueur,
  such as Kahlua
1 ounce (30 ml) Irish crème liqueur,
  such as Bailey's

Cut the avocado into halves longwise. Use a spoon to scoop out the seed. Scoop the avocado into a blender container. Add the condensed milk, 1/2 cup of the milk and enough ice to form a smoothie consistency. Blend to mix. Pour into glasses.

Blend the remaining milk, chocolate syrup, garam masala, coffee liqueur, Irish crème liqueur and enough ice to form a smoothie consistency in the blender. Pour over the avocado mixture. Stir to swirl the layers, then serve.

···IRELAND···

Irish cuisine is commonly misunderstood. The food and cooking of Ireland is richly steeped in history and draws on the wealth of ingredients available from the sea, as well as the beautiful Irish landscape. It's definitely not just mutton and potatoes.

Many influences have made their mark on Ireland and Irish cuisine over the centuries, from the arrival of the Celts in about 600 BC, to the Vikings and the English colonization of Ireland in the sixteenth and seventeenth century.

Like the rest of the U.K. and Europe, Ireland has a thriving modern food culture, and younger chefs have embraced the heritage of their cuisine, preparing it in new ways and elevating recipes handed down over generations to a contemporary standard.

True Irish soda bread remains an international favorite of the Emerald Isle. The original soda breads contained nothing more than flour, buttermilk, baking soda, and salt. Like the young chefs of Ireland, I dressed mine up in its Sunday best and think that you will enjoy this spirited variation.

anardana-flavored irish soda bread

4 to 4 1/2 cups all-purpose flour
2 tablespoons sugar
1 teaspoon salt
2 tablespoons roasted anardana powder (ground dried pomegranate seeds)
1 teaspoon baking soda
4 tablespoons butter
1 1/2 cups chopped dried candied amla (Indian gooseberries)
1 large egg, lightly beaten
1 3/4 cups buttermilk

Enjoy this
spirited
variation
on an
international
favorite of
the Emerald
Isle.

Preheat the oven to 425 degrees. Combine 4 cups flour, the sugar, salt, anardana and baking soda in a large mixing bowl.

Work the butter into the flour mixture with a pastry cutter, two knives or in a food processor until the mixture resembles coarse crumbs. Stir in the amla.

Make a well in the center of the flour mixture. Pour in the egg and buttermilk. Mix with a wooden spoon until the dough is too stiff to stir. Dust your hands with a little flour, then knead the dough gently in the bowl just until it forms a rough ball. Add just a little more flour if needed. The dough should be sticky. Try not to overknead or the bread will be tough.

Shape the dough into a round loaf on a floured surface. Transfer to a greased baking sheet. Use a serrated knife to score the top with an "X" about 1 1/2 inches deep; this helps heat reach the interior of the dough.

Bake for 35 minutes or until the bread is golden and sounds hollow when the bottom is tapped. A long, thin skewer inserted into the center should come out clean.

Let the bread stand on the sheet for 5 to 10 minutes. Remove from the baking sheet and cool briefly. Soda bread is best served warm and freshly baked, but may be served at room temperature, or sliced and toasted. Makes 6 servings.

kokum guinness

If you are unfamiliar with Ireland's pride and joy, Guinness, it may be time to consider upgrading your subterranean digs under that boulder. As one of the world's most beloved brews, this unique Irish stout has that special something that spawns legends. So why mess with perfection? Although truly incredible and delicious on its own, my incorrigible creativity nagged me until I decided to experiment, and the results were extremely exciting.

10 to 12 kokum
10 tablespoons sugar
1 teaspoon lime juice
Pinch of salt
1 teaspoon ground fennel
1 teaspoon ground cumin
1 tablespoon chaat masala
Pinch of asafetida (hing)
Several mint leaves
1 bottle Guinness stout

Soak the kokum in 1/2 cup water for about 1 hour. Combine with the sugar, lime juice, salt, fennel, cumin, chaat masala and asafetida in a food processor. Process until a smooth paste forms. Add 1/2 cup water and mix well. Pour the mixture through a strainer, pressing the pulp to extract the liquid. Discard the pulp. Add the mint leaves to the kokum liquid.

Pour the kokum liquid into a tall glass. Top with the Guinness. Wait for the foam to subside, then fill to the top.

···ITALY···

Given the Italians' unbridled passion for life, love for good food, and significant contribution to world cuisine, fusing an Italian dish was a natural for this book. In Venice I saw how Italians recognize and celebrate their way of life, in which family is a focal point—and the focal point of family is food.

From my experience, Italian households always seem to be humming with energy. It's extended family—the uncles, the aunts, the grandparents—and it's chaos! This is exactly what Indian family is all about. It's about opening your home and having people visiting—everybody taking an interest in your life—everybody treating you as their own—as family. These similarities unite us and inspire me as a chef.

The story of risotto began in the fourteenth century, when the Arabs first brought rice to Sicily and Spain during their rule. Italy's humid weather and abundance of flat lands represented an ideal place to grow this crop, and as a result, Italy is the "rice bowl" of Europe, and rice is an important component of Italian food culture. Risotto has evolved as a core dish of Italian cuisine and a delicious use of this staple ingredient.

At its simplest, risotto is a hearty and elegant rice dish, utilizing the rich flavors of primarily meat or vegetable stock, saffron, Parmesan, butter, and any of the hundreds of possible additions with which it can be paired so beautifully.

Risotto is not only versatile but also easy to make. This has made it extraordinarily popular around the world, from the tinkering of home cooks to the finest restaurants. Here's my version with a slight South Indian twist!

tadka walla risotto

3 tablespoons vegetable oil
1/2 teaspoon black mustard seeds
1/2 teaspoon cumin seeds
1/4 teaspoon asafetida (hing)
1/4 cup chopped roasted peanuts
3 or 4 whole green Thai chiles
1 sprig of curry, leaves removed from stem
3 small onions, finely chopped
1 garlic clove, minced
1 teaspoon minced fresh cilantro
Salt and pepper to taste
2 cups arborio rice
1 cup whole milk
1/4 cup heavy cream
5 cups vegetable stock
1 teaspoon butter
1/2 cup grated Parmesan cheese
1/2 cup grated paneer
Chopped roasted peanuts, for garnish
Chopped cilantro, for garnish

Heat the oil in a large, deep skillet over medium heat. Add the mustard seeds and cumin seeds. Cook until they sizzle. Add the asafetida and peanuts. Fry until brown. Add the chiles, curry leaves, onions and garlic. Cook until the onion is tender and garlic is lightly browned. Add cilantro, salt and pepper and mix well. Add the rice and sauté for 2 minutes.

Add the milk and cream. Heat to a simmer. Add the stock 1 cup at a time and cook, stirring constantly, until it is absorbed before adding more. When the rice is cooked through, add the butter, Parmesan cheese and paneer. Serve hot garnished with additional peanuts and cilantro. Makes 8 servings.

In Italy, family is the focal point, and the focal point of family is food.

limoncello rose

The beginning of 1900 may mark the genesis of limoncello in a small boarding house on the island of Azzurra, where the lady Maria Antonia Farace tended a considerable garden of lemons and oranges. Or it may not, as limoncello's paternity is rife with controversy. People of Sorrento, Amalfi, and Capri all claim that production of limoncello was passed on by various generations.

No matter the beginnings, this deliciously sweet concoction is now enjoyed by many and is a excellent ingredient in an array of specialty cocktails.

1 ounce (30 ml) limoncello
1/2 ounce (15 ml) Campari
2 teaspoons rose syrup
Pinch of ground green cardamom
3 ounces (90 ml) club soda
Organic rose petal, for garnish

Pour the limoncello, Campari, rose syrup and cardamom over ice in a cocktail shaker. Shake vigorously to blend. Pour over rice in a tall glass. Top with club soda and garnish with an organic rose petal.

···JAMAICA···

Upon his return from Jamaica, my husband who is not a big lover of treasures from the sea, came back with tales of a dish with which he was simply enamored—ackee and saltfish, the national dish of Jamaica.

This dish is one that will make even the most seasoned brunch aficionado stand up and clap! Although ackee is a fruit, it is not sweet and is best utilized for savory purposes. When cooked, it quite remarkably resembles scrambled eggs.

The practice of salting and drying cod dates back quite some time, and the resulting fish was an item of international trade between the New World and the Old World. It's used in a vast array of dishes crossing many cultural boundaries.

When the two are put together, along with a healthy sprinkle of my passion for fusion, well, prepare to be delighted.

ackee and saltfish vindaloo

Vindaloo Paste
5 Kashmiri chiles
5 garlic cloves
1 (^{1}/2-inch) piece ginger
1 (1-inch) piece turmeric root
2 teaspoons cumin seeds
1 (1-inch) cinnamon stick
5 peppercorns
4 whole cloves
White vinegar

Fish and Ackee
8 ounces (^{1}/4 kg) saltfish (salted cod)
^{1}/4 cup coconut oil or vegetable oil
2 medium tomatoes, chopped
1 red bell pepper, chopped
1 large onion, cut into rings
^{1}/4 teaspoon ground allspice
Salt and pepper to taste
2 (20-ounce) cans (^{1}/2 kg) ackee,
    drained

For the vindaloo paste, combine the chiles, garlic, ginger, turmeric, cumin, cinnamon, peppercorns and cloves in a blender or food processor. Process, adding just enough vinegar to create a paste.

For the fish and ackee, wash the saltfish thoroughly. Combine with water to cover in a large pan. Bring to a boil. Simmer, uncovered, for 15 minutes. Discard the water and let the fish cool. Break the fish into small pieces, discarding the skin and bones. If the fish tastes too salty, wash it again.

Heat the coconut oil in a large skillet over medium heat. Add the tomatoes, bell pepper, onion and allspice. Sauté until the onion is translucent. Season with salt and pepper. Stir in the vindaloo paste. Add the saltfish and ackee and stir gently. Heat through. Makes 6 servings.

The national dish of Jamaica will make even the most seasoned brunch aficionado stand up and clap!

khus khus thandai reggae

Bhang, an ingredient in many *ayurvedic* medicinal preparations, is made from cannabis and has been used as an intoxicant for centuries. *Bhang Thandai*, a drink native to the Indian subcontinent, is often associated with the *Maha Shivaratri* and *Holi* festival, as it is distributed during this time as a religious offering.

Known to be an energizing and uplifting beverage for hot summer days, it also happens to be extremely healthful and flavorful.

In the west, it is widely agreed that warm weather is a wonderful time to roll out the great rum drinks, and Appleton is one of Jamaica's finest! With that in mind, these two seemed like a match made in heaven.

1 ounce (30 ml) Appleton reserve rum
1/2 cup milk
2 tablespoons sweetened condensed milk
5 blanched almonds
5 cashews
1 teaspoon unsalted sunflower seeds
3 whole green cardamom pods
1/4 teaspoon poppy seeds (khus khus)
2 peppercorns
Pinch of saffron
Crushed ice
Crushed pepper, for garnish

Combine the rum, milk, condensed milk, almonds, cashews, sunflower seeds, cardamom, poppy seeds, peppercorns and saffron in a blender. Process until well-blended. Add ice and blend again. Pour into a glass. Serve frozen, garnished with pepper flakes.

JAPAN

One of my most distinct recollections from childhood is the day when my family stood side-by-side and bid farewell to my father as he set off on a business trip to Japan. He returned soon, and like a messenger with a critical note, he quickly got down to business dazzling us with electrifying stories of his journey, accompanied by exquisite pictures of a land so foreign and exciting, it seemed as if he was recounting a dream.

To no one's surprise, the story that most resonated with me was that of an unusual food culture—unlike any he had ever experienced. This is where my fascination with Japanese food began, and this was my first introduction to the world of sushi. Since then, I have discovered that sushi actually evolved from very meager beginnings over 1,300 years ago.

Fast forward to the 1980s when sushi rocketed to popularity with an increasingly health-conscious population, in America and elsewhere, as one of the healthiest dining options available.

Sushi's appeal has moved from the adventurous eater to the mainstream—it can be found in elegant settings and at the local supermarket. There's just something about sushi that devotees swear is most deliciously addictive.

Sukiyabashi Jiro, Tokyo's famed ten-seat sushi temple, is a great example of how sushi inspires individuals. Global epicurean travelers book tables months in advance and willingly travel thousands of miles to experience the food. A documentary about Sukiyabashi Jiro's honored sushi master and his three coveted Michelin stars is in wide release.

Chefs from all over the world have fused local ingredients into this culinary expression, including the ever-popular California Roll, which features avocado and crab meat. As with any art, sushi continues to evolve as each culture initiates its own experimentation with this ancient craft.

mint cilantro shrimp pakora sushi

Mango Mint Chutney
1 cup cilantro leaves
1 cup mint leaves
1/2 cup chopped mango
5 or 6 green Thai chiles
1/4 cup lime juice
Salt to taste

There's something about sushi that is most deliciously addictive.

Sushi Rice
3 cups short grain rice
1/2 cup rice wine vinegar
3 tablespoons mirin
3 tablespoons sugar

For the chutney, grind the cilantro, mint, mango, chiles, lime juice and salt in a blender until the mixture forms a paste. Add a little water if needed.

For the sushi rice, wash the rice several times until the water is clear. Cover with cold water in a bowl and soak for 20 minutes; drain. Combine with 33/4 cups water in a rice cooker. Cook until the water is absorbed.

Combine the vinegar, mirin and sugar in a small saucepan. Heat over low heat until the sugar is dissolved. Combine with the cooked rice in a large bowl (preferably wooden), mixing well. Cover the bowl with a damp towel. Let stand 30 minutes. Add the chutney and mix well.

shrimp pakora

Shrimp Pakora

$1/2$ cup besan (chick-pea flour)
$1/2$ teaspoon chaat masala
$1/4$ teaspoon ground turmeric
Salt to taste
Vegetable oil for frying
1 pound ($1/2$ kg) 13 to 15-count shrimp,
    peeled, deveined and butterflied

Maki Roll

6 sheets nori
1 cup julienned cucumber
$1/2$ cup julienned red bell pepper
Mint leaves, finely chopped

For the shrimp, combine the besan, chaat masala, turmeric and salt in a bowl. Stir in water a little at a time until a smooth batter forms.

Heat oil in a skillet or deep fryer. Dip each shrimp into the batter to coat thoroughly. Deep-fry until golden brown.

To make a maki roll, lay one nori sheet on a sushi mat, shiny side down. Spread sushi rice over the lower half of the nori to $1/4$-inch thickness. Arrange some of the cucumber and a few pepper strips in the center across the rice. Top with 3 shrimp pakora. Sprinkle with mint. Use the sushi mat to roll the sushi, enclosing the fillings. To seal the roll, use your finger to spread water along the edge of the nori. Press to seal. Cut the roll into 6 pieces. Repeat with the remaining ingredients. Makes 6 servings.

geisha kamasutra

From its origins as the "drink of the Gods" to its current status as one of the most popular drinks in Japan, the history of sake is steeped in both tradition and innovation. Although sake can be traced to China as far back as 4000 BC, it was in the 1300s that the Japanese began mass production and ultimately made popular this simple but delicious brewed rice concoction.

Traditionally, sake is meant to be enjoyed with friends and family. Ancient practice dictates that one must never pour one's own sake; instead, another person pours for you—and you do the same for them. It is this sense of sharing that inspired this recipe.

2 ounces (60 ml) sake
1/2 ounce (15 ml) vanilla rum
1 ounce (30 ml) mango juice
Pinch of spicy Indian curry powder
Splash of grenadine
Mango slice dusted with curry powder, for garnish

Combine the sake, rum, mango juice and curry powder over ice in a cocktail shaker. Shake to blend. Strain into a martini glass. Add a splash of grenadine. Garnish with the mango slice.

···MEXICO···

Churros are a traditional Spanish dessert believed to be developed centuries ago by shepherds living high in the mountains. As you can imagine, in this environment, fresh baked goods were impossible to come by. With tremendous desire comes innovation and experimentation, and the ingenious, nomadic people of the hills came up with the delicious cylindrical, doughnut-like treat known as a churro, which could easily be cooked in a pot or pan over an open fire.

A food as delicious as churros certainly couldn't be restrained by its country's borders for long, and churros arrived in Mexico, likely in the age of the Spanish explorers. Long one of my favorite treats and one that has driven me to many a street fair and festival, the churro lives in my heart as an absolutely timeless dessert. It was a natural impulse to pair this with other flavor favorites, coconut and saffron. What is there not to love about churros? Deep fried, crunchy, sugar, cinnamon—it's hard to go wrong with this scrumptious dessert that is sure to put a smile on the face of anyone who takes a bite!

Deep fried,
crunchy,
sugar,
cinnamon
—it's hard
to go wrong
with this
absolutely
timeless
dessert that
is sure to put
a smile of
the face of
anyone who
takes a bite.

coconut kesari mexican churros

1/2 cup water
1/2 cup coconut milk
4 tablespoons unsalted butter
2 tablespoons brown sugar
1 teaspoon vanilla extract
1/4 teaspoon salt
1 cup all-purpose flour
Pinch of saffron threads mixed with 1 tablespoon milk
4 eggs
Canola oil for frying
1/2 cup granulated sugar
1/2 teaspoon ground cinnamon
1/2 cup dried shredded coconut, toasted

Heat the water, coconut milk, butter, brown sugar, vanilla and salt in a medium saucepan over medium-high heat until bubbles form around the edge. Add the flour all at once and stir quickly with a wooden spoon until no lumps of flour remain. Remove from the heat. Add the saffron mixture. Beat in the eggs 1 at a time with a wooden spoon. The dough should look soft and glossy. Spoon the dough into a pastry bag fitted with a star tip.

Heat canola oil for deep-frying in a large, deep skillet to about 350 degrees, or until the tip of a wooden spoon handle dipped into the oil gives off a slow, steady stream of tiny bubbles. Carefully pipe dough in 6-inch lengths into the hot oil. Fry, turning once, until golden brown on both sides. Drain on paper towels. Combine the granulated sugar, cinnamon and coconut in a paper bag. Close and shake to mix. Put a few warm churros at a time into the bag. Shake until coated. Serve immediately. Makes 10 (6-inch) churros.

corgi coffee atole

Mexico's *atole* is a popular hot beverage/thin porridge made from masa and flavored with cinnamon and brown sugar. When I think of atole, coffee springs to mind. And when I think of coffee, I think of the beautiful rolling hills of Kodagu (Coorg) with its picturesque coffee plantations—a shining star in southwestern India. The interesting part about Indian coffee is that it is commonly blended with chicory, adding a unique flavor. The fusion of these two delicious drinks is one that can be enjoyed morning, noon, and night!

1/2 cup masa harina
5 cups milk
11/2 cups jaggery or gur
1 cinnamon stick
1/2 teaspoon ground black cardamom
4 teaspoons instant Indian coffee powder
2 ounces (60 ml) coffee liqueur, such
  as Kahlúa

Whisk the milk into the masa harina in a saucepan gradually until the mixture is free of lumps. Heat over medium heat, stirring constantly, just until the mixture begins to thicken. Add the sugar and cinnamon stick. Add the cardamom and coffee powder. Heat, stirring vigorously, until the sugar dissolves. Bring to a boil, stirring constantly. Remove the cinnamon stick. Stir in the liqueur and serve hot in mugs.

···MOROCCO···

I savor the time that I can sneak away, if only for a short while, to read about and ultimately explore new cultures.

I was immediately inspired by Morocco because of its similarity to India. The colors, the architecture, and even the food seems so very familiar—yet so different. Like Indian food, the cuisine of Morocco has extremely bold and diverse spices. It is so interesting to see how two completely different parts of the world can evolve in such a similar way.

Moroccan cuisine is a melting pot of many influences, and often you will find Spanish, Arab, Middle-Eastern, and African characteristics. Refined over centuries, the cuisines created in the royal kitchens of Fez, Meknes, Marrakesh, Rabat, and Tetouan ultimately created the basis for what is now contemporary Moroccan cuisine.

The foods and dishes of Moroccan culture take great advantage of the natural resources of the region, and unlike American culture, lunch is considered the most significant meal of the day. The primary Moroccan dish with which most people are familiar is couscous. Chana masala has been a traditional part of the cuisine of northern India for centuries and is as natural a fit for the cuisine of Morocco as jelly is to peanut butter.

moroccan tagine chana masala on couscous

2 tablespoons olive oil
1 pound (1/2 kg) boneless skinless chicken breasts, cut into chunks
1 yellow onion, chopped
6 garlic cloves, minced
2 cups cubed peeled butternut squash
1 cup chopped peeled carrots
1 (16-ounce) can chick-peas, drained
1 (14-ounce) can diced tomatoes in juice
1 1/2 cups chicken broth
1 tablespoon sugar
1 tablespoon lemon juice
2 tablespoons chana masala
1 teaspoon salt
Dash of cayenne pepper
1 tablespoon chopped sweet lemon achar (Indian lemon pickle)
1 cup instant couscous
1 tablespoon olive oil
1/2 teaspoon garlic-ginger paste
1 tablespoon sambar masala
Salt to taste
2 tablespoons chopped cilantro
2 tablespoons toasted sliced almonds, for garnish

Chana masala, a traditional part of the cuisine of northern India for centuries, is as natural a fit for the cuisine of Morocco as jelly is to peanut butter.

Heat 2 tablespoons olive oil in a large skillet over medium heat. Cook the chicken, onion and garlic in the oil over medium heat for 15 minutes or until browned. Add the squash, carrots, chick-peas, tomatoes, broth, sugar, lemon juice and chana masala. Season with 1 teaspoon salt and cayenne pepper. Bring to a boil and cook for 30 minutes or until the vegetables are tender. Add the lemon achar.

Combine the couscous, 1 tablespoon olive oil and 2 cups boiling water in a bowl and mix well. Add the garlic-ginger paste, sambar masala and salt to taste. Let stand until the water is completely absorbed. Fluff with a fork. Add the cilantro.

Spread the couscous around the edge of a serving platter. Mound the chicken tagine in the center. Garnish with almonds. Makes 6 servings.

moroccan mint tea

Unlike Moroccan food, which is primarily cooked by women, tea is traditionally a man's affair and is prepared by the head of the family. It is not only a staple of everyday life, but is also routinely offered to guests as a welcoming gesture. It is considered an insult to the host to refuse.

Westerners seem to love the Moroccan tea ritual. Silvery tea balls packed with green tea are dropped into teapots in preparation for the first contact with steaming water. This first dousing is quickly discarded to "wash" the tea and remove the natural bitterness. Only then is the time right to add a generous serving of sugar and mint leaves in preparation for full immersion, which after steeping ultimately creates the delicious drink that welcomes a guest and promotes fraternization.

A touch of bourbon and ginger liven up the tradition and keep them coming back for more!

2 teaspoons sugar
2 teaspoons Chinese gunpowder green
   tea leaves or other green tea
12 mint leaves, crushed
1 teaspoon fresh ginger juice
2¹/2 cups boiling water
1 ounce (30 ml) bourbon
¹/2 teaspoon ground chaat masala
Mint sprig, for garnish

Combine the sugar, tea leaves, mint and ginger juice in a heatproof bowl or pitcher. Add the boiling water. Cover and let stand 5 minutes. Strain through a fine sieve into another pitcher or large shaker. Add the bourbon, masala and some ice and shake to combine. Pour over ice in tall glasses.

···PERU···

My passion for Peruvian cuisine started with my total obsession with Machu Picchu, just one treasure to be discovered among the country's fascinating history and geography.

Peruvian cuisine is an important expression of its own culture and unique landscape, made up of a vast coastline and the Andes Mountains, which send fresh ingredients and delicious food staples to a wide array of colorful markets.

The culinary history of Peru dates back to the pre-Incas and was later influenced by the arrival of the Spanish. Throughout the years, it incorporated the nuances of a variety of peoples including Spanish, Chinese, Italian, West African, and Japanese.

Fish is a staple in the Peruvian diet and one that is widely appreciated. So it should come as no surprise that a creative selection of ceviches can be found on many menus. The food of Peru is a globally influenced cuisine, and one that deserves to be explored.

fenugreek coriander peruvian ceviche

Fenugreek Oil

2 tablespoons corn oil

1/4 teaspoon dried fenugreek leaves (kasoori methi)

1/4 teaspoon lightly crushed coriander seeds

1/4 teaspoon crushed Kashmiri chile

Sauce and Ceviche

1 yellow bell pepper, seeded and quartered

2 tablespoons aji amarillo paste

2 garlic cloves, minced

1 tablespoon fresh lemon juice

1/4 cup fresh lime juice

1/4 cup clam juice

1 pound (1/2 kg) fresh white sea bass fillets

Soy sauce

1 tablespoon minced cilantro, for garnish

1/2 cup cooked salted choclo or corn nuts, for garnish

For the fenugreek oil, combine the corn oil, fenugreek leaves, coriander seeds and chile and mix well.

For the sauce, boil the bell pepper in a small saucepan of water for 15 minutes; drain. Let cool. Peel off the skin. Purée the pepper in a food processor. Add the aji amarillo, garlic, lemon juice, lime juice and clam juice. Pulse just until combined. Pour the sauce onto a platter with a lip. Chill until ready to serve.

Cut the fish into slices 1/4-inch or thinner. Arrange in the sauce. Use a dropper to drop one or two drops of soy sauce onto each slice of fish. Garnish with cilantro and choclo. Drizzle with the fenugreek oil. It is important to use the freshest fish possible when preparing this dish. Makes 4 servings.

It is no surprise that a creative selection of ceviches can be found on many Peruvian menus.

marigold pisco sour

The pisco sour originated in Lima, Peru, in the 1920s yet interestingly was invented by an American bartender. Victor Vaughn Morris left the United States in 1903 to work in Cerro de Pasco, a city in central Peru. In 1916 he opened Morris' Bar in Lima, which quickly became a popular spot for the Peruvian upper class and English-speaking foreigners and was the birthplace of the pisco sour.

The traditional pisco sour requires Peruvian pisco as the base liquor and the addition of lime (or lemon) juice, simple syrup, ice, egg white, and Angostura bitters.

The marigold is an extremely important flower in Indian culture and is now a widely cultivated crop in southern Asia. Used to make dye, essential oils, medicine, or my favorite, flavoring, the name marigold is a shortened version of "Mary's gold," because the plant was associated with the Virgin Mary. With that said, there is nothing "virgin" about this delicious cocktail.

1/2 cup dried marigold petals
1 cup boiling water
1/4 cup pisco
3 tablespoons lemon juice
2 tablespoons sugar
1 tablespoon egg white
Dash of bitters
1 cup ice cubes
Marigold petals, for garnish

Add the marigold petals to the water in a saucepan. Remove from the heat and let stand for 1 hour; strain. Combine with the pisco, lemon juice, sugar, egg white, bitters and ice in a blender. Blend at high speed until smooth. Pour into two glasses. Garnish with a few marigold petals.

If you are concerned about using raw egg whites, use whites from eggs pasteurized in their shells, which are sold at some specialty food stores, or use an equivalent amount of meringue powder and follow the package directions.

87

···PORTUGAL···

It is believed that *pastéis de nata* were created before the eighteenth century by Catholic monks at the Jerónimos Monastery in Lisbon. During medieval times, it was very common for the the convents and monasteries to use significant quantities of eggs, whose whites were in high demand for starching clothes, as well as used in the clarifying of wines, such as Porto. This created an excess of available egg yolks, resulting in a proliferation of delicious desserts throughout the country. One of Portugal's most famous pastries, *pastéis de nata* is beloved by many, and anyone who ends up in Lisbon will certainly find their way to Pastéis de Belém, widely considered to have the best! Their recipe goes back almost 200 years to the nuns who baked the pastries at the nearby Jerónimos Monastery.

Paan is an Indian tradition in which one chews a combination of shavings of the areca nut, sweetened coconut, rose petal jam, and any of an array of other ingredients according to your individual preference, which are all rolled in a betel leaf. I've taken some of my favorite flavors from this traditional treat and enhanced one of my most cherished desserts—*pastéis de nata!* As you can see in the photo, these are adorned with silvery vark. An edible layer of very pure metal, typically silver, vark is commonly used for garnishing sweets in Indian cuisine.

paan pastéis de nata

16 ounces (1/2 kg) frozen puff pastry
All-purpose flour for dusting
Ground cinnamon
Ground dried coconut
2 cups milk
2 teaspoons gulkund (rose jam)
2 teaspoons butter
1 vanilla bean
1/2 teaspoon ground fennel
1 cup sugar
21/2 tablespoons cornstarch
Pinch of salt
1 egg
3 egg yolks
Sheets of vark
Dried shredded coconut, toasted

Preheat the oven to 425 degrees.

Unroll the puff pastry on a flour-dusted work surface. Cut it into halves. Sprinkle the pastry with a few generous pinches of cinnamon and ground coconut. Roll up each half, starting with the short side. Place in the freezer until firm but not frozen. Cut into 1/2-inch slices. Put a slice into each of 24 muffin cups. Use your thumbs to stretch and shape each pastry so it fills the muffin cup and is flat on the bottom. Bake for 8 to 10 minutes until light golden. Maintain the oven temperature.

Combine the milk, gulkund, butter, vanilla bean and fennel in a saucepan. Bring to a boil. Remove the vanilla bean. Combine the sugar, cornstarch and salt in a small bowl. Add to the milk mixture and mix well. Return to a boil briefly until the mixture thickens. Let cool for at least 10 minutes. Beat in the egg and egg yolks.

Fill the pastry shells half-full of the egg mixture. Bake for 10 to 12 minutes. The pastries should become quite dark on top with black dots, typical for *pastéis de nata*.

To serve, place the vark silver side down over the pastries. Carefully peel the paper backing from the vark. Dust with toasted coconut. Makes 24 pastries.

Created by Catholic monks at at time when significant quantities of egg whites were used for starching clothes, an excess of egg yolks was created, resulting in a proliferation of delicious desserts.

mulled spiced port

With boundaries officially established in 1756, Douro, the area of Portugal known for producing port, is the third-oldest protected wine region in the world. Grapes have been grown in Portugal for thousands of years, at least since the Romans arrived in the second century and produced wine on the same banks of the Douro River where port is produced today.

Mulled wine, called glögg in Sweden, is most commonly made with red wine, port, and brandy simmered with various spices and served hot. A traditional drink during winter, especially around Christmas and Halloween, mulled wine is a chill-chasing favorite with many possible variations. This variation uses port only and adds a luxurious touch of honey that is sure to warm the soul.

1 cup ruby port
1 cup water
2 tablespoons honey
2 whole cloves
2 peppercorns
1/4 cinnamon stick
1 whole red chile
1 star anise
Juice of 1 clementine
1 (1-inch) piece clementine peel
1 (1-inch) piece lemon peel
1 (1-inch) piece lime peel
1/4 Granny Smith apple, finely chopped
Lemon zest strips, for garnish

Combine the wine, water, honey, cloves, peppercorns, cinnamon, chile and anise in a 2-quart saucepan. Add the juice and peel of the clementine, the lemon and lime peels and the apple. Heat until the mixture steams and simmers slightly. Serve in mugs garnished with a thin strip of lemon zest.

···RUSSIA···

When I was just four years old, the demands of my father's job with the steel authority of India called again, and he was sent off to Russia for six months. When he returned, he was bearing gifts and colorful tales of foreign lands. I still remember the beautiful nesting dolls, but even more so, the fairy tale books. These outlined a rich Russian history through folkloric tales that were simply magical and remained my favorites through childhood. As I have always had an insatiable appetite for all things gastronomic, it was the culinary references in the fairy tale books that most captivated me.

While most of our Western food flavors originated in French cuisine, the style of service most of us have become accustomed to is called "Russian service." Plates are delivered to the table pre-filled, as opposed to self-service from communal bowls, known as "family style." Originating from the table of the czar, Russian service caught on very quickly and was so convenient that it is now the primary way we serve our meals at home.

Stretching from the White Sea in the north to the Black Sea in the south, and from the Baltic Sea in the west to the Pacific Ocean in the east, Russia comprises more than 100 different ethnic groups, representing a multiplicity of national histories and cultures, lending to a diverse cuisine.

The food item that Russia is probably best known for is one of our favorite delicacies— caviar! Considered to have originated in Russia, the country can certainly boast the finest in the world. Although caviar was once reserved strictly for royalty, a little known, surprising fact is that in early nineteenth century America, caviar was routinely served during free lunches in saloons. The salty flavor encouraged thirst and enhanced beer sales.

Finally, a bit of Russian table etiquette for your Russian-inspired dish: leaving a small amount of food on your plate indicates that your hosts have provided ample hospitality.

blue corn blini with dal caviar and grape raita

Grape Raita
1 cup chopped black and green seedless grapes
1/2 teaspoon black salt
1 teaspoon toasted ground cumin
1/2 teaspoon chile powder
2 tablespoons chopped mint
1 cup plain yogurt, beaten

Dal Caviar
1/2 cup channa dal, boiled in salted water until tender
1/2 cup green mung dal, boiled in salted water until tender
1 small red onion, minced
1 Thai chile, minced
1/4 cup cilantro, minced
1/4 cup lemon juice
1/2 cup frozen shredded coconut
1 teaspoon sugar
Salt to taste
1 tablespoon canola oil
1/2 teaspoon black mustard seeds
1/2 teaspoon cumin seeds
Pinch of asafetida (hing)
4 curry leaves

Once reserved strictly for royalty, caviar was routinely served during free lunches in saloons in early nineteenth century America.

For the grape raita, mash the grapes slightly in a bowl. Add the black salt, cumin, chile powder and mint and mix well. Let stand for 10 to 15 minutes. Add the yogurt and mix well. Chill until ready to use.

For the dal, boil the channa dal and green mung dal separately in salted water just until tender; drain. Combine the channa dal, mung dal, onion, chile, cilantro, lemon juice, coconut, sugar and salt in a bowl and mix well.

Heat the oil in a small skillet. Add the mustard seeds, cumin seeds, asafetida and curry leaves. When the mustard seeds begin to sizzle, add them to the dal and mix well.

blue corn blini

1 teaspoon yeast
2 tablespoons warm water
1/2 cup blue cornmeal
7 tablespoons all-purpose flour
1/2 teaspoon garam masala
1/4 teaspoon salt
1/2 cup milk
3 tablespoons unsalted butter,
    melted

Combine the yeast and water in a small bowl. Let stand for 5 minutes until foamy.

Stir together the cornmeal, flour, garam masala and salt in a bowl. Add the milk, yeast mixture and butter, whisking after each addition. Let the batter stand at room temperature for about 10 minutes.

Heat a nonstick pan over medium-high heat. Coat with cooking spray. For each blini, pour in 2 tablespoons batter. Cook for 2 to 3 minutes on each side until golden brown and crisp around the edges.

To assemble, spoon a small dollop of raita on each blini. Top with a small spoonful of dal salad. Garnish with additional raita. Serve right away. Makes 16 servings.

siberian blueberry lassi

When the average American pub crawler bellies up to the bar, Russia signifies but one singular libation—vodka. Literally translated as "a little drop of water," Russia's legendary spirit has become the workhorse of American cocktails. In fact, it's the base of the majority of cocktails served up in the U.S. Trendy mixologists aspire to make a name for themselves by putting an artistic twist on this perfectly smooth canvas—at times to much acclaim. However, when the vodka is of a high quality, connoisseurs enjoy it neat.

So, with a chef's perspective, I deliver my splash of spice, developed to transport you to places that should require a passport.

4 ounces (120 ml) organic whole milk yogurt
1¹/2 ounces (45 ml) blueberry-flavored vodka
1 ounce (30 ml) whole milk
3 tablespoons sugar
1 teaspoon rose water
1 green cardamom pod
¹/2 ounce blueberries
Mint sprig, for garnish
Additional blueberries, for garnish

Combine the yogurt, vodka, milk, sugar, rose water, cardamom and ¹/2 ounce blueberries in a blender. Blend until smooth. Chill. Serve cold as an aperitif in a short glass without ice. Garnish with a mint sprig and additional blueberries.

···SINGAPORE···

After a spectacularly successful cooking demonstration at the Singapore Hilton some years back, the local chefs took the rest of us to an extraordinary seafood restaurant very late in the night. It's said that chefs know the best places to eat, and it's true! The restaurant had aquariums floor to ceiling, and you simply pointed to what you wanted and it was prepared for you. This is where I was introduced to the famed Singapore Chile Crab.

Invented in 1950 by Cher Yam, chile crab has for quite some time has been beloved by Singaporeans. The version that is most popular today was modified in the 1960s to include eggs, vinegar, sambal, lemon juice, and tomato paste. This is a dish that is so scrumptious that it earned a place in CNN's "World's Top 50 Most Delicious Foods." Of course, I couldn't let this masterpiece alone, so I added my own personal twist, one that I keep dancing to over and over.

tilwala chile crab

Spice Paste
8 dried red chiles, seeded and soaked
 in hot water
6 garlic cloves
1 (1-inch) piece ginger
1/4 cup ketchup
1/2 cup roasted unsalted peanuts
1/4 cup toasted sesame seeds
2 tablespoons hot chile paste
2 tablespoons dark soy sauce

Crab
1 (2-pound/1 kg) Dungeness crab
2 tablespoons peanut oil
4 green onions, thinly sliced
1 (1-inch) piece fresh ginger,
 peeled and chopped
4 garlic cloves, chopped
1 serrano chile, chopped
2 tablespoons tamarind concentrate
1 tablespoon sugar
Salt to taste
1 tablespoon toasted sesame seeds
2 tablespoons chopped cilantro, plus
 extra for garnish
2 green onions, green portions cut into
 long, thin slices

A dish so scrumptious, chile crab earned a place in CNN's "World's Top 50 Most Delicious Foods."

For the spice paste, combine the chiles, garlic, ginger, ketchup, peanuts, sesame seeds, chile paste and soy sauce in a food processor. Process until very well blended and finely chopped.

For the crab, clean the crab and chop the claws into pieces. Remove the swimmerets and the large claws and chop into six pieces.

Heat a wok until hot. Add the peanut oil. Stir-fry 4 green onions, the ginger, garlic and chile. Add the spice paste and stir-fry until fragrant. Add the crab and 1/4 cup water and stir to combine. Cover the wok and cook for 3 minutes.

Add the tamarind concentrate, sugar and salt. Cook for 2 minutes longer or until the crab meat turns red. Serve garnished with the sesame seeds, cilantro and 2 green onions. Makes 4 servings.

saunf-scented singapore sling

Developed by Ngiam Tong Boon at the Long Bar in Singapore's Raffles Hotel in the early 1900s, the world-famous Singapore Sling is a smooth, slow, sweet cocktail with a complex flavor profile. This sparkling concoction disguises the tartness of gin and cherry brandy, making for an absolutely delicious and memorable cocktail.

Legend has it that this drink was developed in answer to a challenge from a British Colonial's request for a tropical drink that was not only delectable, but befitting the lovely women who were his companions. Saunf, or fennel seeds, provides a further exotic twist that seems like the perfect next chapter in the story of this famous libation.

1¹/2 ounces (45 ml) gin
1 ounce lemon juice
2 tablespoons simple syrup
1¹/2 teaspoons confectioners' sugar
¹/4 teaspoon ground fennel (saunf)
2 ounces (60 ml) club soda
¹/2 ounce (15 ml) kirsch (cherry brandy)
Lemon slice and marschino cherry,
    for garnish

Combine the gin, lemon juice, sugar syrup, confectioners' sugar and fennel in a shaker full of ice; shake vigorously. Strain over ice in a highball glass. Add the club soda. Pour in the kirsch over the back of a bar spoon so it will float on top of the drink. Garnish with the lemon slice and cherry.

···SPAIN···

One of my favorite memories growing up was the breakfast ritual at my home. My mom departed early each morning for her job as school principal, leaving my dad responsible for getting both my sister and me to school. Being completely obsessed with food, I took on the responsibility of being my dad's "partner in crime" in preparing breakfast. This was such a joy—my dad and I would have so much fun performing this task together.

One of the most common items on our breakfast plate was a masala omelet. What made it such fun was that literally anything in the fridge could go into this omelet—no rules. For me, this was extremely exciting, as the experimentation always had my creative engines firing on all cylinders and further fueled my passion for developing new dishes.

Spain's cuisine is greatly enriched by its environment. World-famous hams are cured high in the mountains, vineyards and olive groves sprawl across expanses of beautiful land, and fresh fruits and vegetables are harvested in abundance throughout the country. This abundance is reflected in the traditional Tortilla Espanola, a breakfast favorite that, like my masala omelet, has unlimited variations. I hope that you enjoy this marriage of cuisines.

masala omelet tortilla espanola

3/4 cup Spanish olive oil
6 medium russet potatoes, peeled, quartered and thinly sliced
1 large yellow onion, sliced
Salt and black pepper to taste
1/2 cup Spanish olives, sliced
6 eggs
1/4 cup cilantro, finely chopped
1/2 green Thai chile, chopped
1/2 teaspoon ground turmeric
1/2 teaspoon cayenne pepper
1/4 teaspoon cumin seeds
1 large red onion, chopped
1 (1/2-inch) piece ginger, chopped

A breakfast favorite, Tortilla Espanola, like my masala omelet, has unlimited variations.

Heat the olive oil in a 10-inch ovenproof nonstick sauté pan over medium-high heat. Add the potatoes and yellow onion. Season with salt and black pepper. Cook for 20 minutes or until the potatoes are soft but not brown. Add the olives. Transfer the mixture to a plate using a slotted spoon. There will be some oil left in the pan.

Beat the eggs with cilantro, chile, turmeric, cayenne pepper and salt in a bowl. Preheat the oven to 350 degrees.

Add the cumin to the oil in the pan. When the seeds start to crackle, add the red onion and ginger. Sauté until golden brown. Pour the egg mixture into the skillet, swirling until the egg is well distributed. Add the potatoes to the pan, spreading them evenly. Cook for 3 minutes or until the bottom is lightly browned.

Shake the pan so the tortilla doesn't stick, then slide a spatula along the edge and underneath the tortilla. Put the pan into the oven and bake for 8 minutes or until the eggs are set.

Place a plate over the pan. Invert the tortilla onto the plate. Cut into wedges. Serve at room temperature. Makes 6 servings.

monsoon sangria

Sangria, the word that once meant "blood," is now one of the most popular wine-based drinks in the world. Sangria goes back hundreds if not thousands of years and arguably first appeared in the Iberian peninsula as vineyards became more commonplace. The local resident created fruit punches from the red wines that were readily available.

Fast forward a few hundred years and history was made in the United States at sangria's introduction at the 1964 world's fair in New York City. Now this refreshing concoction, usually made from a base of fruit soaked in red wine, is a delicious drink greatly enjoyed in places far from its origin.

Sangria's potent punch usually comes from brandy, but don't let tradition stop you from experimenting. Numerous other libations can be added and finessed to make your concoction not only original, but the talk of the town.

1 Tulsi tea bag
1 cup boiling water
2 tablespoons sugar
4 ounces (120 ml) white wine
1 ounce (30 ml) blue curaçao
1/2 cup fresh blueberries
1/4 cup concord grapes
1/4 cup sliced plums
1 lemon, cut into thin rounds
Club soda
Basil sprig, for garnish

Steep the tea bag in the water in a cup. Measure out 2 ounces (60 ml) of the brewed tea. Combine with the sugar, wine and curaçao in a pitcher. Add the blueberries, grapes, plums and lemon. Pour over ice in glasses and top with a little club soda. Garnish with basil.

···THAILAND···

In the autumn of 1995 I had just left home to go to college and was confident, being the second of only two children to leave, that my parents would be suffering from an acute case of "empty nest syndrome." Apparently that couldn't have been further from the truth, as very shortly thereafter I received a postcard from Thailand inscribed with the quintessential "Wish you were here!" It must have been a big blow to my ego, but what resonates in my memory are those gorgeous postcards of the Wat Pho in Bangkok with its Golden Reclining Buddha, or the famous Bridge Over the River Kwai. The photographs of Thailand's amazingly rich tapestry of history, architecture, culture, and, of course, food were enchanting.

For those of us in the West, Thai cuisine seems extraordinarily unique—and that it is! Coconut milk, fresh and fragrant spices, lime juice, and lemongrass create a signature sweet and sour taste—something that is not reflected in Western dishes. A longer look at the history of the region reveals that Thai food has been heavily influenced by the fare of its neighbors, along with the cooking habits of the missionaries and other outsiders that came to the region. These, along with the unique fresh ingredients, have combined to create a national cuisine that is truly an original.

A typical Thai dish comprises four main seasonings: salty, sweet, sour, and spicy-hot. In fact, most Thai dishes are not considered satisfying unless they combine all four tastes.

Interesting Thai myth: After a meal, there is no such thing as dispensing with leftovers. Throwing away food is believed to enrage the Thai "god of rice," a female deity who watches over the people, ensuring everyone has enough to eat.

Interesting Thai fact: Most people do not know that Thai is not a chopstick cuisine.

paneer tadka pad thai

$1/2$ pound ($1/4$ kg) rice noodles
3 tablespoons tamarind concentrate
3 tablespoons fish sauce
2 tablespoons brown sugar
$1/4$ cup peanut oil
$1/2$ teaspoon black mustard seeds
1 teaspoon sambar masala or
    curry powder
$1/4$ teaspoon asafetida (hing)
$1/4$ cup crushed unsalted peanuts
3 or 4 green Thai chiles
3 curry leaves
Salt to taste
$3/4$ cup firm paneer, cut into cubes

4 or 5 garlic cloves, finely chopped
3 shallots, thinly sliced
$1/4$ cup chopped sweetened salted radish
1 teaspoon peanut oil
3 eggs
3 cups fresh bean sprouts
1 cup garlic chives, cut into $1^1/2$-inch
    segments (optional)
$2/3$ cup chopped unsalted roasted
    peanuts
4 green onions, trimmed and crisped in
    ice water
A few short cilantro sprigs, for garnish
1 lime, cut into wedges, for garnish

Soak the rice noodles in cool water in a bowl for 40 minutes to 1 hour; drain.

Combine the tamarind concentrate, fish sauce and brown sugar in a small bowl.

Heat $1/4$ cup peanut oil in a wok or skillet. Add the mustard seeds and cook until they sizzle. Add the masala, asafetida and crushed peanuts and fry until browned. Add the chiles, curry leaves and salt and fry for 2 minutes.

Add the paneer and cook until golden. Add the garlic and stir-fry briefly. Add the shallots and stir-fry for 15 seconds. Add the radish and mix well. Heat through for a few seconds. Add the noodles and toss to coat. Stir-fry until most of the noodles have softened.

Push the noodles to one side of the pan. Add 1 teaspoon peanut oil. Add the eggs and scramble to blend them as they cook. Break up the cooked eggs with a spatula. Add to the noodles and toss to combine.

Add the tamarind mixture and mix well. Add 2 cups of the bean sprouts and the garlic chives. Sprinkle with half the chopped peanuts. Cook, stirring, until the sprouts and chives have wilted.

Serve on a platter or in individual bowls garnished with remaining sprouts, remaining peanuts, green onions, cilantro and lime wedges. Makes 4 servings.

thai masala martini

Martinis come in such a wide variety these days, and creativity seems to be the name of the game. In inventing a cocktail that fuses the aromatic beauty of Thai cuisine and the spiciness of India's fare, the first flavors that came to my mind were lemongrass and garam masala. This fragrant concoction is appropriate for any season and is sure to satisfy that South Asian travel itch. Best of all, it will have your guests demanding seconds!

Lemon grass tea
1 stalk lemon grass
2 kaffir lime leaves
1 (1-inch) piece fresh galangal

Martini
1 1/2 ounces (45 ml) vodka
1/2 ounce (15 ml) simple syrup
2 tablespoons fresh lemon juice
Pinch of garam masala
1 small chunk ginger, peeled
1 stalk lemon grass, cut into pieces
  for garnish
4 thin ginger slices, for garnish

For the tea, boil the lemon grass, lime leaves and galangal in 1 cup water in a saucepan; strain and chill.

For the martini, combine 4 ounces (120 ml) of the tea with the vodka, simple syrup, lemon juice and garam masala in a shaker filled three-fourths full of cracked ice. Shake for 1 minute, then let stand for 1 minute. Rub the chunk of ginger on the insides of frozen martini glasses. Strain the martini into the glasses. Garnish each with a piece of lemongrass and a ginger slice.

···UNITED STATES···

There is nothing that quite says American food like the good old-fashioned hot dog. Growing up in India in a really, really small town by the name of Ranchi, my exposure to American food was limited to what I read in *Archie* comic books. I was spellbound when Jughead would go to Pop Tate's and consume these huge, amazing-looking burgers and shakes—a tantalizing vision for the blossoming foodie.

The origin of the hot dog is vague and in dispute, but the idea of a hot dog on a bun is ascribed to the wife of a German named Antonoine Feuchtwanger, who sold her creations on the streets of St. Louis, Missouri. Customers were usually given a white glove for holding and eating the hot sausage. She hit on the idea of a bun to replace the white glove when customers kept walking off with the gloves.

Over the years my love of cooking compelled me to try and re-create hot dogs and fries as I first envisioned them. When the time came to fuse some of my favorite tastes into these dishes, I had an epiphany if you will—an inspiration that has delighted many! The fact is that many Indians do not eat beef, hence the term "Holy Cow!!" Even McDonald's does not serve a beef burger in India. In its place is the Shahi Burger (royal burger), which is made from ground chicken. More inspiration came from friends who had returned from America and opened a fast-food, vegetarian American restaurant. Aptly named "Yankees" and highlighting an array of interesting vegetarian burgers, this opened my eyes and gave me ideas, so I started to experiment. I present my homage to the classic American hot dog!

malai chicken hot dogs

Mango Mustard
1 cup mustard
1/2 cup mango pulp
1/2 teaspoon dried mint
1/2 cup minced mango

Chicken Hot Dogs
2 pounds (1 kg) ground chicken
1/4 cup cream cheese
1 tablespoon grated garlic
1 tablespoon grated ginger
2 eggs, well beaten
1 teaspoon kasoori methi
1/4 cup tandoori masala

2 small red onions, finely chopped
2 jalapeño chiles, grated
1/2 cup chopped mint
1/2 cup chopped cilantro
1/4 cup chopped ginger
Butter
8 brioche buns
Mayonnaise
Mint leaves
Granny Smith apple slices pickled in
    apple cider
Jalapeño chile slices pickled in
    apple cider

My homage to the classic American hot dog.

For the mango mustard, combine the mustard, mango pulp, mint and minced mango in a bowl and mix well.

For the hot dogs, combine the chicken, cream cheese, garlic, ginger, eggs, kastoori methi, tandoori masala, onions, chiles, mint, cilantro and ginger in a large bowl and mix well. Form the mixture into hot dogs. Sear over high heat in a skillet until cooked through.

Put a dot of butter onto each bun half. Grill them cut side down until golden. Assemble each serving with a bun, hot dog, mango mustard, mayonnaise, mint leaves, apple slices and jalapeño slices. Serve with Tandoori Onion Rings (recipe follows).

tandoori onion rings

Onions are probably one of my favorite vegetables. I love them raw, sautéed, caramelized, fried—you name it. One claimant to the invention of the onion ring is the Pig Stand restaurant founded in Oak Cliff, Texas, in the early 1920s. At its pinnacle, this once-thriving chain had over 100 locations across the United States. On the other side of the world, in India, one of my favorites growing up was a very popular dish called Pyaz Bhaji, which essentially is onion fritters. This interpretation is a melding of the two—a more westernized version with, of course, the addition of Indian spices!

Onion ring masala
1 tablespoon toasted cumin, ground
2 tablespoons chaat masala
1 tablespoon ground red chile
1 tablespoon dried mint

Onion rings
1 cup buttermilk
1 tablespoon tandoori masala
2 large onions, cut into $1/8$-inch rings
2 cups all-purpose flour
Vegetable oil for frying

For the onion ring masala, combine the cumin, chaat masala, red chile and mint in a small bowl and mix well.

For the onion rings, combine the buttermilk and tandoori masala in a large bowl. Add the onion rings and toss to coat. Refrigerate, covered, for 1 hour or longer.

Heat oil in a deep fryer. Combine the flour and 2 tablespoons of the onion ring masala. Coat the onion rings in the flour, shaking off any excess. Fry the onion rings in batches for about 3 minutes until golden brown, turning to cook evenly. Drain on paper towels. Season with more onion ring masala.

nimbu pani mint julep

The Mint Julep is an iconic cocktail that in many ways defines the romance of the American Southeast. It seemingly became popular in this area's agricultural regions, where farmers would awake at dawn. Originally a morning drink, the Mint Julep was used as a spirited equivalent of coffee in today's society. However, I am quite sure that like me, many of you were first introduced to this fabulous drink by one of my favorite films of all time, *Gone With the Wind*. Today this American classic is closely associated with the world-famous Kentucky Derby, where a whopping 80,000 Mint Juleps are now served up during the course of this much anticipated and celebrated annual event.

I was inspired to pair the Mint Julep with Nimbu Pani, an Indian lemonade. Also known as lemon water, this is a refreshing thirst quencher and can commonly be found in Indian homes on those scorching hot summer days. Variations on this form of lemonade can be found worldwide, and no matter its use, like the Mint Julep, it's always greeted with a thankful smile.

Mint Black Salt Simple Syrup
1/2 cup sugar
3/4 teaspoon Indian black rock salt
1/2 bunch mint, leaves removed from stems

Julep
2 juicy limes
Mint leaves
Club soda
2 ounces (60 ml) good-quality Kentucky bourbon
Mint sprigs, for garnish

For the simple syrup, combine 1/2 cup water, the sugar, black rock salt and mint leaves in a small saucepan. Simmer over medium heat until the sugar and salt dissolve. Chill in the refrigerator. Strain, discarding the solids.

For the julep, squeeze the limes into a pitcher. Add the mint simple syrup. Crush or muddle a few mint leaves in an 8-ounce julep cup until the mixture forms a paste. Fill the glass half-full of crushed or shaved ice. Add the lime juice mixture, club soda and bourbon. Stir until the outside of the cup is frosted. (A glass tumbler will not frost on the outside.) Garnish with fresh mint.

···VIETNAM···

Steeped in a rich history, the food of the Vietnamese is one of the jewels of Southeast Asian cuisine. A blend of certain ingredients and traditions of classic French food and a selection of Chinese and Asian spices have resulted in a wide array of delicious and uniquely flavored dishes.

Vietnamese baguette sandwiches, called *banh mi*, have developed an almost cult-like following of epicurean devotees. The bread used in these delicious sandwiches was introduced by the French during its colonial period in Vietnam and is usually more airy than its western counterpart—so as a result, the banh mi has a thinner crust. This envelops the choice array of potential fillings in a most delectable and delicious crunch!

My first *banh mi* experience was fairly recent. I had heard of this amazing sandwich many times and then became obsessed with trying the best and the most authentic *banh mi* available in the U.S. After trying *banh mi* in a few different cities, I discovered my hands-down favorite right in my own backyard—New York City's Chinatown. I love the crunchiness of the baguette, the fresh bite of the daikon and the unapologetic spiciness of the jalapeño chiles.

Banh mi characteristically includes very flavorful meats, so India's classic tandoori chicken seemed like the perfect fit. Marinated in yogurt, lemon juice, and plenty of spices, then grilled or broiled, this was a match made in heaven!

chicken tandoori banh mi

1 daikon radish, peeled
1 carrot, peeled
1/2 cup unseasoned rice vinegar
1 tablespoon sugar
1/2 teaspoon salt
2 tablespoons vegetable oil
1 tablespoon fish sauce
1/2 teaspoon soy sauce
1 (24-inch) soft baguette
2 tandoori chicken breasts, thinly sliced (recipe follows)
2 jalapeño chiles, sliced
1/2 sweet onion, cut into 1/4-inch rings
3/4 cup (packed) cilantro
Lettuce leaves
2 tablespoons mayonnaise

Preheat the oven to 350 degrees. Place oven rack in the middle.

Cut the radish and carrot into ribbons with a peeler. Stir together the vinegar, sugar and salt in a medium bowl. Add the radish and carrot and mix well. Let stand, stirring occasionally, for 15 minutes.

Combine the oil, fish sauce and soy sauce in a small bowl. Heat the baguette in the oven for 5 minutes or just until crusty. Cut off and discard the round ends. Cut the baguette into halves lengthwise. Brush the bottom slice with the oil mixture.

Drain the radish slaw in a colander. Arrange the chicken, slaw, jalapeño, onion, cilantro and lettuce over on the bottom of the baguette. Spread mayonnaise on the cut side of the baguette's top half. Top the sandwich. Cut into four pieces. Makes 2 servings.

Banh mi have developed an almost cult-like following of epicurean devotees.

tandoori chicken

3 tablespoons vegetable oil
1 teaspoon ground coriander
1 teaspoon ground cumin
1 teaspoon ground turmeric
1 teaspoon cayenne pepper
1 tablespoon tandoori
   masala
1 cup plain yogurt
2 tablespoons lemon juice
4 garlic cloves, minced
2 tablespoons minced ginger
1 teaspoon salt
4 chicken breasts

Heat the oil in a small pan over medium heat. Add the coriander, cumin, turmeric, cayenne pepper and tandoori masala and cook for 2 to 3 minutes until fragrant, stirring often. Cool completely.

Combine the cooled spice mixture with the yogurt in a large bowl and whisk to blend. Add the lemon juice, garlic, ginger and salt and mix well. Add the chicken and stir to coat with the marinade. Chill, covered, for at least 1 hour and up to 6 hours (but no more than 8 hours).

Heat the grill. Remove the chicken from the marinade, shaking off any excess. Grill the chicken until cooked through. Let stand for 5 minutes before slicing.

pomegranate falooda hột é

When basil seeds are soaked in water, they puff up and become gelatinous. Called Hột é in Vietnam and *Falooda* in India, this delicious drink is consumed *en masse*. In India, falooda is a cold and sweet beverage containing any of a wide array of additional ingredients including items like rose syrup, vermicelli, jelly pieces, and tapioca pearls along with either milk, water, or ice cream. As you can imagine, there are quite a few interpretations of this delicious concoction. I have taken some liberties with this alcoholic version, but the key ingredient and texture enhancement of basil seeds remains intact and is sure to deliver a pleasant and delicious sensation.

2 tablespoons basil seeds
1/4 cup superfine sugar, or to taste
2 tablespoons honey
1/2 cup fresh Meyer or regular lemon juice
1/2 cup pomegranate juice
2 tablespoons ginger juice
2 ounces (60 ml) citron vodka
Fresh basil leaves for garnish

Wash the basil seeds in a large strainer under running water. Place the seeds in a pitcher. Bring 2 cups water to a near boil in a saucepan. Pour over the basil seeds. Let stand for 5 minutes for the seeds to expand.

Combine 2 cups water and the sugar in the saucepan. Bring to a near boil. Stir in the honey until blended. Pour into the pitcher.

Combine 2 ounces of the basil seed syrup, the lemon juice, pomegranate juice and ginger juice with the vodka and ice in a shaker. Shake to blend. Pour into glasses and garnish with basil leaves.

index

index

spice index

spice index

The more unusual ingredients found in some of the recipes
are readily available at Indian markets, which can be found in
most cities. If you'd rather order online, we highly recommend
the following two Web sites:

www.kalustyans.com   www.theethnicgrocer.com

To purchase additional copies of *Flavors of My World*, call 800-358-0560 or visit www.maneetchauhan.com.